AF323928

Embedded Alive

Embedded Alive

First Person Journalism in the United States of America

C. G. Braswell

Library of Congress Control Number 2014947560

ISBN: Hardcover   978-0-9906-741-2-2

             Softcover   978-0-9906-741-0-8

             Ebook   978-0-9906-441-1-5

First Edition

Gorham Printing, printer

Kimbriel, K. E., editor

Braswell, C. G., author

Portions of this work were originally published in *Modern Times Magazine.* Author photo courtesy of Randall Murrow Photography. Special thanks to the Federal Bureau of Investigation; the United States Senate; the Attorney General of Texas; the Office of the Arizona Governor; Joseph J. Kubacki, Sergeant At Arms, Arizona State Senate Capitol Complex; the Sheriff's Office of Cochise County, Arizona; the Department of Philosophy at the University of Texas at Austin; the University of North Texas Mayborn School of Journalism; *Modern Times Magazine* and J.D. Guzzon; the *Scott Horton Show* and Scott Horton; Sifu Wallace Cupp; the Insight Meditation Center in Redwood City, Calif.; the United States Army; and J.G. and E.R. Braswell.

To order additional copies of this book, contact:

Braswell Communications Inc.

1-713-409-3017

www.fusepowder.com

chris.braswell@fusepowder.com

Table of Contents

Preface

All journalists should eventually get good enough at their job as to become unemployable in important ways. That is good news, and it is how it worked for me. I am somehow paying the rent and feeding the family, but I am not doing it without some form of charity or suffrage, tacit support, and a certain amount of blind faith. Even if held incommunicado or in solitary confinement, no one can get by totally alone, without the onset of rot, death, or insanity. That is why hermitage, which I have explored in some of its lesser modes over the years, seems to result in such a mixed bag. Even solitary animals must come together some times.

An awareness of the importance of community is why I still feel obligated to make civil responses to in-bad-faith situations, even if they do not involve me. But it is a lonely position at times, because altruism really does not seem to pay in the jungle; rather it is viewed as a weakness. At sea, there is arguably greater clarity to such high ideals as the notion that we are all part of a singular, larger thing, and when parts of it are ill, all constituents must suffer for it without escape. This all may present positive moral implications about mariners and people like them, but anyway, the law of the sea and the law of the jungle are distinctly apart.

Righting or reconciling oneself with one's surroundings involves understanding one's own worth, role, and context in the at-large marketplace of ideas. As for my specific vocational training, I suppose the service value I provide can be categorized in various ways that include being a denizen of an ad hoc or at-large vocational guild, as it were, which, more broadly speaking, can be categorized as art (apropos literature), information service (reportage), education (through forensic journalism, web logs, editorials, letters, and public speaking) and entertainment (pseudonymous fiction and live music).

I have plenty of worthwhile hobbies and various democratic duties too. I am a parent, a musician, a neighbor, a camping enthusiast, and a citizen, with a college education and a lifelong academic track, on paths in the contemplative and martial arts, and with faith-based volunteer commitments among other things. Such activities provide ambient benefits to the community at large. For example, I have extensive experience giving care to infants and children; I have the spiritual charms of a chorister and the philosophical eagerness of a willing and would-be theosopher. And if need be, I can ward off threats or physically defend myself or other people using bare physical force. I can hastily write fiction, I am fair at composite sketching and pretty good at voice-over audio production. I play the saxophone and the steel-string guitar. Also, at times I am irritable, nearsighted, self-centered, don't have much of a social life, and often listen to the same old records over and over again.

These days, I am increasingly interested in a wider range of media, e.g. audio and drawing/sketching. However, the pen is still the primary implement and a faithful companion, and this book is a backlog of some of my non-fiction content. My reader here finds me a decade after college, which followed eleven years in the restaurant service industry, and at all times I am receding from the art of bagging groceries at age fifteen.

~CGB, July 28, 2014

Opinion and Editorials 2013-2014

After finishing college I paid some dues as the cub reporter for a daily newspaper in an Army town in the U.S. Desert Southwest. That took about four years. Then I went to work in the corporate sphere, and eventually I was thrown from the cubicle saddle. Now I am a self-employed scrivener by my own election; I have brought my craft home. I office at home, and at all hours of the day and night. When I leave the house, I am still at work. When I meet people, or when strangers judge me, their predispositions about writer types usually determine the nature of our relationship. As such, damn near all of my relationships fit into one of two categories: either strictly business or anonymous.

Writing the fiction is fun, changing the ribbon on my typewriter is cathartic, the editorial production and marketing process is a nice diversion, and trying to piece together the world and its solutions is rewarding because such efforts have value and merit.

That ethic is part of the key now. I am no longer just writing down what I saw, or what the exact authoritative details were for a particular automobile accident. While continuing to accumulate historical perspective, I am now working with eyes that have grown more generally specialized, and I frequently find myself in a position to see things that others may not see, and react through my writing in a way that only I am able, for the purpose of shedding light on a subject, or explaining the fundamentals of a problem, or even bringing about beneficial change through action and awareness.

In the past couple of years, as my eye has continued to grow stronger in its faculty, and I become increasingly effective with my quill, these editorials have come about during the course of my daily work. They are not perfect, but they represent right effort.

~CGB, January 8, 2015

Class Action Illumines Digital Currencies and Boundaries of Privacy

January 22, 2013

Litigation has made its way to the United States District Court for the Northern District of California in San Jose, escorted by a proposed settlement of $20 million for Facebook Inc.'s apparent non-consensual use of its account holders' names, profile pictures, and identities for the social media website's advertisements.

Fraley v. Facebook, Inc., 966 F. Supp. 2d 939 (N.D. Cal. 2013) is timely in helping reinforce an emerging digital currency system. Digitally, linking to your friend's poetry or mentioning the address of your brother's firm may not involve the exchange of script, notes, or paper, nevertheless a transaction in good faith has essentially occurred. It is increasingly recognized that this sort of activity has real market relevance and equity. In fact, such networking is the capital coin of the electronic realm where the value of a community is generated and defined entirely by its constituency. It is a proactive, encouraged form of networking and is comparable to friendly word-of-mouth advertising. Such a legitimate form of new money can be thought of as incumbent old money.

Generally, anything else is widely recognized as dubious and unwanted solicitation at best. Spam, phishing, spoofing, and other such online trolling is how squatters, con artists, and other interlopers attempt to gain a toehold in people's neighborhoods, networks, system architectures, and lives.

It is important to define and retain the appropriate physical boundaries and context among the concepts of property, privacy, right of way, value, and exclusivity, regardless of the situation at hand. Simply because an activity is opportune in one venue and is not so in another ("there is no rule against it") does not define the ruling ethic nor should it govern behavior. And, if something seems harmless after the fact ("people will get over it"), such retrospective apologetics do not expressly denote ethical behavior nor is it a useful way to define community terms. These are the kinds of questions about ethics that must be constantly addressed by responsible parties in order for a community to allow a free range of motion in a given marketplace, while functioning autonomously and existing exclusively from other communities and rights of way.

It is important that the substantive issue is not outshined by the digital medium being evaluated. Just like any other community, whether digital or analog, it is up to Facebook's user community to define itself and set its rules. If a person does not want her personal account to be involved in business-to-business advertising, it would probably be wise for her to select something besides the Facebook network when she chooses social media clients. Also, Facebook is not the Internet. We must avoid the ad hominem fallacy that stems from confusing the digital medium at large for specific modes therein. For the purposes that Facebook currently serves, such as for viewing photographs of one's former classmate's children, the tracking and profiling of sociological demographics and behavior, business-to-business advertising, cottage-industry marketing, and as a general chatter box, it is apparently successful. A caveat that must be made here is one of principle, though the company apparently did not ask or disclaim (presumably now it does) that it would use individual personal accounts as corporate advert mules, e.g., the "Sponsored Ads" as described in the lawsuit.

Conversely, corporate Facebook accounts and public figures welcome this sort of ambient marketing atmosphere. What is ad clutter to one community is ad support to some other.

Sent to potential class members, a notification of the Fraley v. Facebook settlement said that the company denies any wrongdoing and any liability. It also says that no other court or regulator has made any judgment or determination of liability regarding this issue. The case could set a legal precedent and have some role in defining the legal landscape of the digital world. With that, it is germane to the welfare of our at-large marketplace of ideas.

Fine. And remember, Facebook is not the Internet. It is many things, including an excellent starter kit for peer-to-peer social networking, but it is not alpha and omega.

On a digital chip, modern life's expectations are much the same as life in, say, an often smoggy but frequently-decent residential neighborhood in west Houston. If the community suspects that a crime has occurred or is occurring, or if something that the community has defined as a crime occurs in plain sight, there is an obligation for the community to mobilize and intervene, thus compromising the criminal's freedom and head space. And as on the neighborhood block, so on the web. But beyond that, generally, there is a reasonable expectation of privacy; and unless you have specifically authorized otherwise, people cannot view the contents of your underwear drawer, watch you undress, enter your dwelling, or take your belongings.

I or my pseudonymous aliases may like kickboxing for example, but the local mixed martial arts gym cannot not hang signs on the front gate of my home without permission, and arguably neither can the landlord nor the city of Houston. Further, these organizations cannot advertise in my name(s) without my expressed consent.

Similarly, an electronic mail address is privileged, sensitive, personal information, and it can be compared with a residential address in that it should not be disseminated to anyone who you would not suffer as a dinner guest, at the least. For this common sense reason, among many others, the practice of providing electronic mail lists of individuals to third parties is extremely dangerous. As with real property, information related to the access of intellectual property is extremely sensitive. Mindful examination and clarification on the subject, when the opportunity arises, is critical.

French existentialist philosopher John Paul Sartre used the term "abandonment" to "describe the absence of any sources of ethical authority, either in religion or from an understanding of the natural world," according to the *Oxford Companion to Philosophy, 1995*. In the present mid-morning of the 21st century, we face an enabling and inspiring reality of opportunity in this increasingly integrated digital-analog hybrid world. Concurrently, many of us are coming of age in our own right judgment and find ourselves so empowered, standing on our own upon such a plateau. Now is our time to appropriately define our communities, define our market terms, "valuate" our currencies, groom and police our intellectual gardens, cover our losses, and capitalize our well being.

Objects in Wallet May be Larger Than They Appear

February 20, 2013

Something is wrong with the currency system. Or to phrase it more accurately, the currency system is mismanaged and misunderstood. This is not the worst of news, though, because such things can be corrected.

There is a misunderstanding regarding the ethic that fundamentally underwrites the United States dollar (that is, regarding how actual value is correlated to symbolic coinage or paper script notes.) The currency represents particular ideals. It has no significant worth unto itself, rather, it carries or denotes a value. It serves to both entitle and obligate the currency bearer in particular ways. People do not bear capital equity in their own right, except perhaps if considered strictly in terms of livestock. However, to use actual laborers and artisans as legal tender is not an ethically equitable proposition. It is even further afield to say that a person engenders more equity in the marketplace than another person simply because she carries more script. That would be to say that she is more enfranchised in the marketplace because she possesses a larger "bill of goods." That is a fallacy, and people who would tell you the currency works in such a way are failing to understand how it works, or, are trying to manipulate you and the marketplace in bad faith.

One does not use twenty-five wrenches to tighten one bolt, and a hammer hanging on a hook does not drive nails. Currency is worthless anytime it is not being exchanged in a marketplace. Yes, this means currency is useless when it is being collected in great volumes in puffy banks or being buried in coffee cans instead of being used as guaranty in transactions or agreements.

A deal, exchange, or transaction is either equitable or not equitable. If a market situation is equitable, then someone may or may not elect to underwrite it with currency, and in doing so, the situation is proposed as marketable. Essentially, the *ideals* that in turn underwrite the currency system are intended to invoke or preserve the conditions which must exist to facilitate a fair deal in good faith. These circumstances include open communication, common understanding, mutual trust, and honesty regarding terms. The currency also invokes certain ideals about what is a good climate for investment, such as certain prerequisites for sustained market activity ("this transaction is not going to injure me or debase the marketplace"), optimism ("tomorrow will come bearing new opportunities"), helpfulness ("my or your product is worthwhile"), service ("let's negotiate instead of cheat or steal"), hope ("I am happy that the system functions and provides opportunity"), amity ("I enjoy conducting business with you, business is fun"), and adventurousness ("business activity is legitimate and worthwhile, this new product is good").

No value-based system correlates value with meritless products or services, irrational propositions, intractable contracts, or illegitimate operations. The dollar has a bullish disposition by design as a result of its prescription for brokering only right transactions that are made in good faith. The currency underwrites the transaction in which it is being applied. This stabilizes the market right-of-way that is shared among the parties involved in a conversation or agreement about the exchange of goods or services. One of the dollar's sell-side functions is as a tool with which to enfranchise market activity, by allowing goods or services to be exchanged in the light of a symbolic guaranty in good faith. One of its backside roles is that its presence bears a standard of philosophical faith in the mettle of the market itself.

So, the currency is intended only to be encountered in marketplaces where the involved entities have already agreed, by formal caucus or informally as a community, upon its meaning and value. It follows that the currency invokes or represents a type of common law contract. Therefore its bearer or bearers play a critical role in deciding what products, services, and business locations are determined to be acceptable for retaining designation in a currency's market realm. Do not assume, just because you transact using currency at a given location, that other people are there doing likewise with the same currency in the same good faith; you may be the only one. Do not presume that other people are using the same currency system, nor that others understand your system as the tool it is. Do not assume that others' systems are underwritten in the same way as your system. But if someone is using the dollar, then any U.S. citizen has an ethical interest in the transaction, with determinations about the nature and degree of that interest being qualified as a function of common civil law (such as American constitutional law) regarding natural liberties. It may be a private debt, but the dollar is a public contract.

Consider this publishing project, for example. The business model is designed to get the book to market, in the context of a number of sociological factors, value systems, and cultural benchmarks. The primary role of the project is the dissemination of ideas. I am the staff. There is a protocol in place for handling revenue, but it is secondary to the project's main goal. So the business model is not configured to rapidly generate revenue without some meaningful end, as a virus would attempt to replicate itself in a host system for no other reason than simply to multiply itself for the sake of multiplying. Enterprises with such a misplaced goal in mind have missed the point regarding what currency means and is. The attainment of currency cannot be a philosophical goal or objective (barring some sort of test or experiment about currency). Currency is not real property, it is a tool. (It is a type of intellectual property, yes, but then we're off into a discussion about republican ideals and democratic citizenship.) One of the tool's appropriations is to help enfranchise business in a marketplace, for example, but it is not an end unto itself as a commodity.

It is important to know with whom one is sharing a currency system (if anyone), because sharing the system or even using a common model amounts to a true partnership and even partisanship. A partner's actions with the currency, in very real ways, bind all of the system's users to the agreements underwritten and any consequences thereby. This does compel a person to scrupulousness and shrewdness when engaging in business activity, so as not to lose one's effective business partners in exchange for inferior ones or none at all. It also puts cause upon community members for intervention at times when the currency is misappropriated or misapplied. Birds of a feather flock together, so the saying goes, and the notion of a public contracts weighs heavy in human culture.

This is where currency management meets community management, whether active or passive. For example, I would never recommend that anyone purchase any kind of lottery ticket. Furthermore, I do not wish to share a currency system with anyone who purchases lottery tickets and defines it to be a reasonable investment. Therefore, I have a compelling argument advocating for my own economic protection in the marketplace at large, from people who purchase lottery tickets with dollars. If old friends of mine wish to purchase a lottery ticket as some sort of novelty, barring forensic purposes, I would be very interested to hear their proposed logic as to why such a transaction is beneficial or equitable.

In essence, lottery players are attempting to underwrite a contest to reach "high" "values" attached to a bill of goods, on behalf of themselves and their potentially unsuspecting peers in the marketplace. This sort of activity debauches a currency system, because it is not an equitable opportunity and cannot be underwritten in good faith. Furthermore, it is dubious and impeachable when institutions, organizations, or people collude to enable or encourage this sort of misappropriation or proliferation of misunderstanding or disinformation not in good faith. For me, any lottery involvement begins and ends with a boycott, based on my understanding that purchasing lottery tickets is a waste of my good time, a poor investment on behalf of myself and the people with who I may now or in the future share the marketplace at large, and a weakening of the currency tool itself. I do not recall entering into any contract whereby I condone the accommodation of habitual lottery players' ticket purchasing habits, or the regular purchase of such things in place of perhaps a much more direly needed bus ticket to a 12-step meeting, for example. If I have somehow given such consent implicitly or otherwise, then I recant herewith.

Yet, as of Monday, the Ohio Lottery's Classic Lotto "jackpot" was $27.9 million. The Powerball was about $50 million on Wednesday. So apparently someone, somewhere, is doing preposterous things with their dollar. People or organizations who demonstrate any such irresponsibility (such as buying lottery tickets or holding lotteries) or misunderstanding (trying to cash a bill, defrauding people or abusing the tool by claiming that a bill of goods has real property value), precipitate a force majeure market situation that must result in the reduction or elimination of their enfranchisement in the marketplace. This protects the marketplace, its ethical operators, the system itself, the citizenry, and its liberty.

The Perils and Penelopes of First Principles and the Stigmata of Symbolism

April 1, 2013

Symbols are philosophically powerful because they can communicate an entire world of information instantaneously.

For example, the swastika is an ancient figure and the word has a Sanskrit *(स्वस्तिक or svástika)* etymology that translates as "lucky charm." The typical Hindu version has a dot under each arm. From the Indus Valley and throughout the globe, for thousands of years, the swastika adorned buildings, clothes, and jewelry.

On the other hand, a black swastika in a white circle on a red field became the flag of the National Socialist political party, and the activities of the German Reich brought about a stigma to the symbol that was far afield from what had been its historical meaning. Such stigmatization of a symbol compels interesting questions about dynamics of control, proprietorship, and management within the marketplace of ideas. It also encourages investigation of various symbols and their meanings, and the surveying of those meanings in their own light and aesthetic context.

Another example: The arrangement of the rainbow bars of the color spectrum represent not just the light in the visible physical world, but also the frequencies of energy that are above and below the visible band; comprising altogether both the seen and unseen of the vast cosmos. The swastika and the pride flag are examples of how stigmatization of a particular symbol engenders a formidably heightened robustness of the symbolic vehicle and its intended or original meaning in the marketplace of ideas. Generally, the power of symbols is due to their potential for communicating an entire universal wealth of knowledge in a flash. The source or cause of the power is the knowledge itself, as well as the practicality of its vehicle of transmission. As they denote pure ideas, symbols are a powerful vehicle. A logo is about as close as one can get to bottling an idea, barring chemical nanoengineering. As such, people may be willing to go to great lengths to occlude the epistemology of certain symbols, and even so far as to generate disinformation. In fact, it might be wise to perhaps double-check regarding what one may have been historically led to believe.

Chain of Custody in the Marketplace of Idea

When one receives information, it is wise to think very hard about whether it is coming from its source, or second-hand from an information broker. Symbolism is helpful in the evaluation of vectors and integrity in the marketplace of ideas, for example with respect to propaganda, advertising, and public service. Such forensic analysis illumines origins and trajectories of information, as well as its corruption or deviance. Such investigations are useful in all walks, i.e. criminal justice, sociology, economics, civics, and, ahem, history.

When the actual cause or origin of a symbol or of any other information or phenomenon, is successfully isolated the situation can be considered in its own light and aesthetic context in order to reveal fundamental philosophical truth and its implications.

A "banks failing" scenario is a study in the power of symbolism and regarding the chain of custody of ideas or information in a marketplace. One may realize that "banks failing" is not caused by an accidental systematic or systemic flaw or by untenable market parameters, but instead by intentional sabotage or inept administration. Then upon considering the consequence in light of the actual cause, it might become obvious that instead of "banks failing," what actually happened was that "a targeted cabal was successfully liquidated," or perhaps "a story about banks failing was fabricated in order to occlude the fact that the banks did not fail." In that light, it would be useful to consider questions such as: Who told the story about banks failing? Or who might have wanted them to fail? Or who might have wanted them to appear to have failed in order to help ensure that they continued to operate?

If a currency by definition facilitates economic marketplace activity in good faith, then upon re-evaluation of the original "banks failing" story, it can be understood that certain parties likely exist such as: Those who actively support market activity that is or could be underwritten in good faith; Those who believe that such good faith market activity is imperiled to such an extent that espionage and black operations are warranted in order to protect parties who are vested in the free market, and; Those who are not operating in good faith and whose behavior after the fashion warrants their removal from the marketplace by parties who are vested therein.

The Art of Quitting

April 15, 2013

The time of Lent makes for an effective tool for letting go of bad habits. Upon quitting something for six weeks, one finds it much easier to quit it permanently, and that is why people often use this window of piety and frugality on the Christian calendar to do such "spring cleaning."

By the time Easter arrives, the consideration is no longer "should I quit," but "should I start," because burial of the habit is already begun. It is comparable to an academic track: one may or may not elect to attend graduate school, but she cannot even so much as apply without the requisite undergraduate course work.

I have ceased many bad habits in the convalescence of my 30s. About the turn of the last century, as I was pulling away from the motley era of my early 20s, I was encouraged to get into the gym by the owner of a tavern where I worked. At that, I began a renewed attention to my physical regimen and diet, which had been neglected since the end of eighth grade football. When stripping away bad habits, a person can always find more fundamental ones laying in the wait, and it only makes sense to start with the big obvious ones, because if those aren't extinguished, the subject cannot get at (and often cannot even perceive) the ones buried more deeply.

As Lent 2013 began, first I decided to give up baked sweets, because I was chowing down pastries and chocolates in obvious compensation for having given up caffeine (except for perhaps a cup of hot green tea every several months) and sodas in 2011.

I also decided to pass on various meats for Lent 2013.

I had been reading the Third Book of Moses that contains Judaic laws of antiquity, which are today still the only pertinent laws for a very many people. It is my understanding that the gnostic advent of the Christ was a green light for things like tattoos, which had been historically forbidden by the old law. However, for a number of reasons, I took a real interest in what the patriarch wrote about food. In doing so, I was joining a community which I was interested in becoming a part of, for the sake of needing to belong somewhere, among other reasons. Further, although I was already historically mindful of diet, I was interested in how the decision might help me to capitalize on the results of my physical workouts and personal preventative health maintenance, which these days have become rather advanced (or simplified, depending on one's perspective). The experiment was also part of my ongoing efforts to better manage my finite physiological energy resources, which are in high demand as a parent, professional, and writer.

The long and the short of it is that I was a full-blown, permanent vegan by Easter.

An important factor of meat cessation is a logistical argument. One has obligations to be extremely cautious in situations where one's indirect actions in the marketplace correlate directly with factors of supply and demand, and to the logistical web not just at the point of sale but also upstream and downstream of one's activities. Individuals are answerable to the consequences of what they, whether individually or collectively as part of a community, may set into motion or perpetuate (or prevent or change or allow) when transacting in a market. Regardless of whether *caveat emptor* is posted anywhere nearby, its truth remains.

A person can be mindful of diet, yet still never be

confronted with a decision regarding consumption of animals. But any contemplative, methodical, holistic, and persistent attempt to isolate and remove any non-beneficial or malignant practices or feedstock invariably precipitates meat cessation. Once it has begun, the first habits to go relate to one's own mouth. Following such an initial personal clearing of the palate, one typically begins to look outward to whatever greater geographical, sociological, and distribution network they live in. It is the sort of closer consideration typically encountered by intensely dedicated people such as professional athletes, soldiers, scientists, academics, monastics, and home-school teachers.

At first, I decided to stop eating chickens, turkeys, pigs, and shellfish, though I originally planned to keep going with the other fish, some cows, and other cow-like animals, all of which I had been making a concentrated effort to minimize over the years anyway. But it did not last, and very soon I was part of a kinship, among the herbivorous dinosaurs of the Stone Age as well as the dreadlocked produce department staffer at the nearby market. I have tried this before, and it didn't last. This time it did take, probably because now a more healthy, daily lifestyle foundation is already firmly in place (compared to that of, say, my historical self as a less-clean-living college undergraduate who patronized smoky bars and regularly stayed up too late, among numerous other unhealthy habits).

Ideally, if one does not personally produce the food he eats, then he ought to be personally acquainted with the people who do. In this way, there is no space for error or mystery in the logistical chain, as its operational management and knowledge management occurs from beginning to end among market constituents in the open air of a known community.

If immediately verifiable oversight or auditable logistics of such a nature is not in place, even if there is just one gap in the chain, then the entire operation becomes a total mystery from every perspective. The producer does not know his end-user consumer, and the consumer does not know who produced his food or how so, not to mention who transported it. With just one such blind spot, any point within the intervening logistical chain is exposed to a completely blind alley. But any one alley is infinitely too much, when it's blind. And, with an extremely complex logistical web with multiple blind alleys, for example, such as that marshaled by someone living in greater metro Houston who wants to eat a chicken in the next five minutes, it should be obvious that the probability of something going badly wrong is quite perfect. That person gets their chicken or "chicken" in no time, by compelling the economy by way of writ (in this instance, the passing of paper money) to meet their demand on the Texas Gulf Coast for such a meat immediately. But a non-negotiable demand, if it is a technically (i.e. ecologically) intractable demand for a given time and location, will require a logistical chain that is questionable at best. Emptor is what he eats.

Pet food is a good example of the awareness problem here. Typical dog food is obviously not fit for human consumption, and that should be fine because we are not eating it. Problem solved, right? No, not logistically, and not in other ways either. If you don't know where and who the salmon and turkey and cows in the cat food are coming from, the potential problem remains, alley cats and all. Even if you do, it still presents and ethical problem.

Who killed the chicken, how, and where? Was it farmer Joe next door or a robot? Chickens require space, and without that space, they are not just friendly yard birds, they are insane, shit-covered, caged animals on death row. Who cleaned the machine that filled the plastic hummus container with hummus? Was it farmer Ted's son, or was it a laborer with whom you are not acquainted? Who grew the beans? Who drilled the oil, or cut down the tree, to make the container and where did they get the land or ocean or forest with which to do so? And was this all done in your name using your currency? Would it be better if it were done by masked strangers using alien means?

It is an issue that is beyond just meat, or just food. Anything that has a logistical trail which is complex enough to have been shipped, packaged, sold in bulk, produced in bulk, painted, loaded, stored, sprayed, frozen, boxed, dried, stamped, or inspected is part of an extremely complicated logistical process where clear oversight must occur. The same conversation can be had for the logistical wake downstream of your role as a consumer or retailer, and should be pondered every time one flushes a toilet. Luckily, water, thus sewage, is valuable and is worth properly handling and storing; but that is an article for another day.

A good step in the right direction: Get to know the truck drivers who deliver goods to the markets you patronize, both food and non-food related. They have more answers than one might think, and can help. Find out how knowledgeable your drivers and store managers are regarding the origin of their goods, and if they appear ignorant or negligent, report them to their managers and corporate offices. And if those managers are dodgy, report them to the press and community leaders, and alert your friends, neighbors, and partners in the area. Also speak up if your local community leaders aren't acting right. Often they are really trying to help, but sometimes they are the last ones in the way of efforts clearing blind alleys.

Sometimes you find that no one knows or cares but yourself, in which case, congratulations, you are now a community leader! I suggest you keep a notepad and pencil handy at all times, perhaps one that fits in your back pocket.

If you're like me, you might treat the meat department like a perpetually fresh homicide scene. Try it, imagine the yellow tape in your mind's eye, and pay attention to who's behind and in front of the counter, just as a mental exercise, and let me know if it helps put your community and its members into a clearer perspective.

We all must be careful regarding what sort of activity we support by our patronage in the marketplace. Start by asking questions to help generate awareness for yourself and others. If you don't know, asking simple questions are better than not thinking about the issue or not trying to help at all.

Context and Census of Intellectual Marketplaces

May 3, 2013

The scope and quality of content in a given marketplace of ideas is essentially determined by its constituency. The ideas generated, maintained, and protected by a community's denizens are the legal tender in such a thoroughfare of thoughts and thinking. Without the exchange or generation of ideas, there can be no such sustainable venue of minds. A closed market of ideas that is advertised as free and open is a fake, and usually is a killing floor. And if a constituency is few, or naught, or it is neither creative nor thoughtful, that particular situation also cannot be defined as an intellectual thoroughfare.

Qualification and Factions

Naming a given constituency and its members is necessary to sustain a healthy thoroughfare of ideas. It is key to any organized effort at sourcing the origins of ideas and enabling a constituency to manage its marketplace. Any individual also has a responsibility to identify her own resident marketplaces, roles, and associates in the intellectual rights of way. Every thinking person should be actively engaged in paying attention to the tides and flows of thought and thinking, to the well-being of venues used by thinkers, and to one's own context therewith.

An organized effort at clearly defining the full parameter of intellectual rights-of-way provides for analysis of the venue's arrangement among various sociological ontologies. Examples are: Other market venues, schools of thought, institutions, individuals, and known ideologies. Such critical consideration enables more effective management, navigation, and understanding about a given thoroughfare of ideas.

All open markets are potentially connected and can be viewed as one universal venue. It is important to remember that there is a multiplicity of distinct or specialized marketplaces; e.g. science, engineering, literature, and fine arts, or books, theater, religion, and civics are all full-blown categories in their own right of the faculties of thought. A constituent demographic that comprises one marketplace will be unique compared to any other market community. Content-specific factions, intellectual guilds, or at-large subject matter experts among different communities can enhance universal interactivity among diverse markets.

Quantification and Attribution

Resourcing of individual members enhances the general accessibility of the core knowledge base in an intellectual community. The constituency of any intellectual marketplace should be empirically immanent as it is the incumbent source of ideas and systems of thought. The members of an intellectual community should be obvious.

From beginning to end, if the source of any information or campaign is not plain to see, down to its respective progenitor(s), then there is a problem, a potential for extreme danger. A source of information and ideas must be accessible and candid in order to be authoritatively referenced for the sake of understanding, veracity, clarity, posterity, and oversight in knowledge building.

If an idea which does not clearly stand on its own merit is unsourced, unreferenced, unattributed, or otherwise carried without a sufficiently disclosed context, then it lacks systematic rigor and should therein be deemed unfit for use in the exchange or transmission of thoughts and ideas in a free and openly functioning platform of critical thought. Clandestine origins bear an inherent dubiosity of subclinical trajectories and goals. Such veiled modes do not abide by the format of verifiability that is required of any rigorous, open-table venue of thinking.

There is an intrinsic inter-connectivity that all free markets allow, in order to sustain and enrich productive exchange among minds in building upon universally established knowledge. As such, an interloper in an intellectual marketplace can have perilous implications for all domains that function in good-faith support of the free exchange of ideas.

A big problem in the management of intellectual rights of way occurs when people conflate their ideologies when defining the "world and its parameters," which is basically just another idea within some greater marketplace of ideas. Meanwhile, one way to define an idea is to think of it as a "world crafted in its own right."

So a mindful marketplace constituency should be relied upon to quickly point out, that at a very fundamental and essential level, "worlds" in and of themselves can be logically defined as "ideas." There is more than just one world and worlds are quantifiable in an organized system of ideas. Further, "ideas" can flower into and often do comprise entire worlds of thought and reality. Ask any writer, any librarian, any artist, or any philosophy major. Ask yourself.

A quantified, qualified constituency in an open venue precludes any culture of confusion regarding sources, veracity, and content, and allows for the immediate identification and response to clandestine and thus potentially malignant sources.

Hazards and Goals

Because the consumption of ideas is a critical function for communications among constituent marketplace agents, I have engaged over the past decade in subjective tests involving abstinence from various mediums and ideological campaigns. Through this subjective media blackout, there are a number of highlights, such as:

1: There are hazards. One example is the abundance of vaguely sourced information regarding community management, at the ground level and very close to the edit. Another example is the notable, predictive, and recidivist misinformation and obfuscation that prevails among various distinct realms of content. The subject of the latter example would be information which has been established historically, through critically rigorous protocols of learning and knowledge exchange, and are otherwise known among empirical communities to be inarguable axiomatic parameters of closed systems.

2: Most if not all of the hazardous vectors are obvious. Certain modes of ideology can have a predictive negative influence upon the vivacity, geography, and constituency of any intellectual marketplace. That is why these modes must be policed by design against subversion, which is harmful to critical thought and universal creative processes and impedes the sovereignty of individuals and open tables of discourse. Two such major restrictive vectors are immediately apparent. One vector is the control of access by, to, and for particular constituents, modes, groups, or markets. The other vector is the imposition of an ideological parameter from which any deviance is punished or quashed, or any parameter otherwise that prevents the free perusal and exchange of thoughts, ideas, and qualified knowledge.

3: Some things are certainly something, but they are definitely not open intellectual thoroughfares. An ideological marketplace and an open venue of thought are not the same thing, and an ideology does not denote an intellectual marketplace. There are some venues with no constituency at all, or at least not containing what we would qualify as legitimate jurisdictions of critical thought or innovative and complex dialog or conversation. Therefore, there are implications about the definition of a constituent and marketplaces of various kinds. If there is no definable thinking constituency then there is no definable venue of thought. Such landscapes should be well marked in order to prevent tepid, undesirable quackery from destroying healthy, working thoroughfares of thought and collaboration.

It is an intellectual comeuppance to realize the difference and to depart from such dark places hence never to return. There may be many such autonomous philosophical deserts or wastelands, present through contrivance, neglect, and mismanagement. They are big vapid holes; boondoggles that should be avoided. Historically, the sociological zoology regarding ideological constituencies is much more than just a cottage industry. Enjoyed by many, it is a political pastime unto itself. Many artful efforts have skillfully defined, analyzed, and criticized the constituencies of various ideological realms, often taking the shape of allegorical satire in literature and art, such as Pink Floyd's tenth studio album, *Animals*, created in 1977, and George Orwell's allegorical novel *Animal Farm*, written in 1948

The "stick" that we are trying to avoid, is the destruction or degradation of our realms of dialog, discourse, critical analysis, and thought exchange, in a modern and worldly technological setting where, unfettered by such clutter, the sky has proven to be the limit. Provided with the tools and intellectual resources available now, to achieve thriving venues for thought exchange is ultimately a reasonable and plausible goal in essentially any field or school of thought. Successful examples of which are many, to include the Internet Archive, Wikipedia, the Open Source Initiative, and various independent media communities and artisans' guilds.

The "carrot" we strive for, are sustained intellectual marketplaces which are free of unproductive, cumbersome, unsolicited clutter, bad information, and anachronistic content such as e-mail spam, unwanted ad clutter, malware, antiquated propaganda ideologies and vectors, and fruitless and untimely functional constraints. In a properly functioning right of way, it should be a cinch to isolate and correct such problems.

Work: Defining (What is Not) Equitable Labor

July 23, 2013

So far in 2013, some of the editorial pages herein have featured ongoing philosophical discussions about symbolism and currencies, marketplaces of ideas, economies, supply and demand, market demographics, and census.

Service to these various subjects has maintained an overarching theme about the importance of operating in the context of good faith and right equity in order for systems to function practically and appropriately. But it is impossible to consider all of the aforementioned aspects of our world without also considering the relevance of "labor" in the same critical light as we have addressed the previous topics.

Bearing in mind that one of the modern uses of currency is a symbol of value attached to goods or services in a marketplace, in order to preclude the actual use of laborers and artisans as legal tender, then something is wrong when a currency does not reflect the heart and objective best interest of its underwritten workers. Perhaps the clearest editorial angle here is to observe what labor and work are not, in order to more closely approach the heart of the question.

Currency and Work: Ethically Representing the Value of Labor

When communications or transportation infrastructure is built privately in good faith, and subsequently its holders contract its use to people in a marketplace, who 1) wish to use it to communicate signals, and, who 2) do not possess their own such infrastructure, then, the situation appears to qualify as a simple two-party service agreement that reflects the interests of both the owners and users of the infrastructure.

But, if any market transaction is not a strictly in-kind transaction exchanging goods and/or services, and subsequently it involves any currency which does not have a clear, overtly stated, representatively-exact value of what is being exchanged, then a major economic philosophical problem manifests. That is, in one sense, a currency floated or constituent to a given transaction should have a one-for-one value exchange rate with respect to the value of what is being tendered, in order that the transaction can be thought of as occurring in good faith.

Either 1) a fair deal closes, or 2) a loan is made and a debt created. A transaction cannot be both. Currency is a key element in a non-slave labor force; currency must be underwritten or guaranteed for it to represent the actual value of goods or services and such value can only be attached to a currency through direct correlation with either goods or labor capacity or the labor force itself.

Erroneous Conflation of Representative Valuation

Another example: A government builds (or authorizes) a railroad on state land. Its engineering and technical maintenance is performed by certified technicians at large, and the operating model is structured to conform to environmental and market parameters, all in good faith. All of this seems to be a legitimate culmination of an effort by the labor force, provided that the materials, rights of way, and personnel are soundly applied.

For an organization to exchange for, or agree to buy or rent, logistical railroad right-of-way for its own business purposes is one thing. However, for an organization to procure logistical railroad right-of-way in order to exchange it for the purposes of "cash profit" on a market is not an act of equitable labor, and it's also not a proper application of any currency tool. "Cash profit" is, in essence, a nonsensical term, particularly if the profit sought is of and by the same units of currency that underwrote the development and maintenance of a respective asset. Profiteering is a counterintuitive use of the intellectual tool, and it is a kind of racketeering which is a crime, and it is a vector frequently used for the intentional destabilization of a system or community. An operator cannot capitalize where in a domain where there is no common wealth.

Financial fraud in general is an assault against a marketplace and a crime against those vested in it. It does not represent the conscience of the labor force, moreover, it is not work or innovation. In fraud, nothing has been innovated, no new service vector has been enabled, and nothing has been made easier through any such activities of an entity that is operating as nothing more than a holding company if not an economic parasite.

People involved in such business are not performing "work," that is, they are not apparently acting in good faith for the benefit of the market, or for the providers of goods or services, or for the currency tool that represents said providers, or the community. Such behavior only serves to damage the economy, the efficacy of the currency, and the vested parties it represents, which includes the labor force.

To allow such a transaction is an abandonment or shortfall of a natural regulatory aspect of an economy, enabling detachment from equity and value in certain operating sectors of an economy. The actual work and its representative agreements that were involved with the development of the infrastructure and technology simply is not interchangeable or exchangeable with any debauched, after-the-fact, derelict currency-derivative script brought into being by transacting goods and services for profit, instead of goods and services for other goods and services. To transact for profit destroys the value of the asset being "profited" from, and thereby degrades the economy to which the asset was constituent.

Conflating two such definitions of "currency" (labor-value-equitable currency versus derelict currency derivatives) causes inflation (that is, value-equitable currency is ruined, among other negative consequences, and thus labor becomes disenfranchised from its own strong suit). Such monetary profiteering is the most perfect example of an assault against a labor force and an overall economy that I can conceive of.

Where they are allowed, such holding companies and transactions must ultimately be stopped; and their perpetrators and enablers are welcome to try and find a star system, somewhere far from here, where their dung-heap economic philosophy would be given quarter by some mysterious people who do not mind having their labor-representative currencies mucked up. Go tax yourself. Either that, or it is a bold-faced and malicious assault against a system, that should be quickly dealt with right here on our local rights-of-way.

Strong-Arm Theft, Burglary and Coercion, Road Agent Solicitation

As a general rule, the committing of crimes or doing anything else in bad faith is not equitable work. Theft of goods, materials, and services is not honest work. Robbery is not an act of equitable labor. Clandestinely generating fiscal liquidity through the spoofing of billable accounts is not work. Beating or killing people or animals or the destruction of property without cause is not equitable labor. Simply duplicating or creating facsimiles of currency script is not an act of equitable labor; rather it is an assault on the economic system, its labor force, and anyone vested in the market. Currency replication for its own sake is as fruitless and misguided as are panhandlers who ask for coins instead of asking for food and shelter.

There is much talk about currency on this page because a currency represents the labor force and its collective spoils or common wealth, and so it carries a direct correlation with the gravity of the labor force in a given market. So any appropriation of the currency that is not in the best interest of the market and its constituent labor force is neither appropriate nor justifiable, and it is always grotesquely suspicious at least.

Another example of what is not work: Someone else's work is not one's own work, even if a person decides to say that it is; and also not because that person wrote down somewhere that they had decided, that although it was not, they nevertheless wanted it to be theirs so therefore it was theirs. Someone else's work is also not one's own work simply because some mud-covered asshole from out of state was compelled to pen purple prose describing someone else's efforts or results of equitable labor as not its original author's but rather the thief's own. A reasonable person might expect that there is no reason to iterate what seems to be such a common sense distinction. However, as it turns out, it must be carefully shouted among certain company, that such activities do not count as equitable work in good faith. Ask any enlightened person who understands the holistic transcendence of time, space, morality or ethics, and equity, and she will communicate to you that each and every instance of such attempted intellectual property theft stands to be studiously attended to and gloriously corrected with extreme prejudice.

A final example of what work is not: Transacting to buy or sell the personal contact information for individuals or groups of people, for purposes such as marketing or sales, is not an equitable appropriation of billable personnel hours. This type of chicanery is not "work" and it does not serve the market, moreover the purported ends to such activity in a marketplace do not generate equitable value. The only worth enjoined by such practices involves forensics and intelligence, and to describe it as anything other than either 1) a means to do honest good-faith police work, or, 2) the creation of a vector for identity theft on a massive scale, is to tell a big fat lie that has gone out of your rattling brain-pan through your horrible lying mouth and right into someone's nice and soft, undeserving ear holes who probably do not like being lied to, ever at all.

Such acts are typically done without consent from, or even open two-way dialog with, the victims whose information is being bought and sold for resale. This particular racket is a black bull market that thrives via widespread abuse of implied consent. Those whose information is bought and sold are victims of the crimes of identity theft and privacy violation. This intimacy is not to be trusted to "sales associates" foreign or domestic, because the only "value" such activities provide to "sales associates" is that of a vantage from which to attack the position of market entities, whether they be specific businesses, particular constituencies, market factions, or sociological demographics. There is no place for such malicious, clandestine, in bad faith activities in an open, good-faith market where clear and apparent equity of a labor force and its livelihood is the patent emblem.

First Pillar, Second Sight, Third Angle, Fourth Estate, Fifth Column

June 24, 2013

Fiction writers are the type of people who understand that fictional characters can surprise their creators by manifesting very real personalities and psychologies of their own. And not just sometimes, and it is not always subtle. Such characters are the stuff of pure imagination, and they bear real presence and volition that can go far beyond the designs of their creators.

For example, certain friends of mine now only will refer to me as Detective Rick Thompson of the Washington State Police. Thompson was the protagonist in one of my pseudonymous novellas. The stereotypical noir police detective battles grimy street urchins and supernatural threats, and only after publishing did I realize how intimately these ciphers correlated to historically protagonistic and antagonistic characters and positions in my own life's story. Regardless of my intent, these fictional entities illuminated portions of my own back pages that may have otherwise remained occluded from me forever.

That is catharsis; it is successful, self-induced, accidental psychotherapy. To be a scrivener and to realize one's intimacy with characters of his own creation, as well as unexpected and equally robust intimacy with one's audience as the stories move and inform readers' lives. Thereby; living out the ongoing growth and maintenance of a writer's personal faculty and public station; seeing the unfading watermark of an established writer's voice; finding firm wherewithal as an author and creator of art through writing; and finding acceptance among an age-old guild to grow in a timeless craft. These are among the lures that enable the retention of the demanding and challenging muse of literary creativity and those who persevere therewith.

But give the writer a stage, and put him in the company of a nimble drama team, and he is confronted with previously undiscovered opposable thumbs to use in his literature, through her artistic sister, theater.

My casting in the St. Luke's United Methodist Church Tapestry Player's Summer Stock Theater production of Kaufmann and Hart's *You Can't Take It With You* was a special moment in my career as a writer. For example, among so many other insights, I was struck by the valuable access that the stage provides to character psychology. Simply put, it is much easier to create a character when you have breathed for him.

Moreover, the production was an effort that bears very strong spiritual equity for all of the people involved, to include the audiences. Such truly legitimate work is priceless for its inter-demographic, inter-generational nexus; for its strengthening of bonds; and for its opening of new and positive dialog among the brotherhood and sisterhood in Christ.

Dramatic theater functions as an institution within the community, and provides a vehicle for a community to reference itself, ensuring that no item of importance is overlooked and that no old business blocks any path where hatchets are buried. And we are all better off for it.

Live theater readies and reinforces the framework for leaps of faith in our everyday lives, including the ones that can be taken by the players at any moment during a live production. Theatrical productions strengthen people and reinforce communities. Its crucial role becomes even more obvious when it is beheld from the vantage of the stage.

Take Me To Your Lender

July 1, 2013

We drove the streets and alleys on the backside of our new rental home yesterday after church. Back there, which is to the east, is an area of mixed zoning, with high density housing, some light industrial, and some office / business commercial areas. There is also a full radio communications tower installation, which I suppose would be heavy industrial zoning, within 150 yards of this property. North of us is contiguous single-family residential zoning for about two blocks before it yields to the commercial clutter of a minor east-west arterial thoroughfare. South of here is single-family residential up to another minor east-west arterial right of way, the south side of which gives way to high density residential zoning that is within 1,000 yards of the westbound Katy Freeway / Interstate 10 right of way. West of here are several square miles of posted homeowners association domain comprising single family residential zoning that is contiguous with that of the property my family occupies. The neighborhood abuts a major north-south arterial on its west side.

I did not see any direct evidence of narcotics use or narcotics culture unlike in Westchase District, where we recently moved from, so there is more successfully applied integration here than in our old neighborhood, along those lines. The area is obviously better policed by its occupants, which is good news.

So, behind the property where we live (to the east), much of the office business infrastructure (which is not visible from our backyard because of trees) seems to contain residential tenants, among other operations that do not seem to be functioning as any sort of open business.

Numerous and various window blinds are visibly crumpled up from the inside, as the spaces are crammed full of undetermined stored items. In and about the business lots is significant pedestrian traffic that would typically be indicative of an area of high-density residential zoning.

In the parking lot of one particular light-industrial / business-office property back there is an old General Electric sign, and a Harris County Precinct One Constable's Office logo-painted trailer that appears to be an automated radar-enforcement unit of the sort typically used to monitor the speed of traffic. On this lot, as I drove through, I could see storage units in the building, visible from the right of way, with vertically opening garage-style slide doors. One of these was open, revealing a storage space quite jam-packed nearly full by length and height of stored items. There was one small space cleared inside on its west edge, that led back into its interior, at the front of which there was a chair by the door where sat a woman holding a plastic hand-held toiletry mirror. It must have been her home.

Back there in a nearby white-brick apartment tenement there was not much visible activity, but for one male-female couple apparently preparing to load partially constructed furniture into a large pickup truck. Virtually all of the parking spaces were occupied by a number of apparently functional vehicles which would indicate a tenant population of far, far more than the building size would seem to have accommodated at full occupancy.

I would also note, when I jog through the neighborhood to the west of our rental home, that certain various of the single-family residential lots appear to have their outside appearances kept up although upon second glance, they do not bear the typically apparent nuances of houses that are lived in by people who are regularly coming and going during the course of typical domestic affairs (for example there are no vehicles, or they have constantly occluded windows, or there are trash accumulations of the sort that a resident so attentive to the landscaping would also likely remove, or some go so far as to have contrived "still life" yard affectations in a futile attempt to achieve a "lived in" look, etc.). There was a similar sort of phenomena in the residential area of the Westchase District. There appear to be simply huge numbers of empty yet unmarked houses in multiple regions throughout the city. Who or what are the parties who put forth that the housing market is tight and booming? What cabal is sitting on this real estate at the peril of the community and the market? On its face, it would not appear to be an investment in good faith. Why are houses being built? What could be the exact recipe of contractor fraud, mortgage and bank fraud, and broker fraud that is in play here?

There are at least three yard-work contractors who apparently live within one block of us in the immediate neighborhood area, I think they just mow all day and squat all night, and repeat. Not the ones on my street, of course, but other different ones who don't live so close to me. There are various general contractors doing various sorts of work on empty / unoccupied houses in the neighborhood, either gutting and cleaning homes for remodeling, or otherwise bringing some or another unoccupied home into repair. Considering that a significant number of the homes in the neighborhood are empty, I wonder what was going on with ours before we moved here? Who knows. Obviously all the paint, glass, and fixtures are new. Even if it were not out of my "price range," I would not build a new one, wasteful as it would be with all of the empty better ones everywhere. It's the same way with office space, where it often is in use as housing, or it is empty.

The situations in the areas behind this lot on the east side of the house beg questions such as: to whom are the business district's residential occupants paying rent? Who is accepting payment or are these just squatters? And if they are squatters, what sort of business or property management tolerates squatters at or near its properties? Under what or whose terms are these agreements conducted, and with what sort of currency or guaranty? A few of the people in my neighborhood seem to be keeping familiar business hours, but most seem not. There are implications here regarding currency value and market economics. Am I the only person or one of the only people in the neighborhood who is occupying the economic system as I have come to understand it? Maybe I do not understand, after all. Am I the only one who is not answerable to a slum lord, or, am I instead realizing that I *am* answerable in such a way, in fact?

If my currency is so valueless as to be completely disregarded by the global market around me, then what generates the demand for it? What factors are the cause of its scarcity, at the peril of my business' operation and domestic maintenance? Barring some unknown, velvet-handed, ethically compromised coin-counting imp, I am confounded. If the currency now represents such a representative worthlessness, why is there still demand for me to pay rent and bills specifically with it? What would be the source of actual demand for currency if not some representation of actual value? Why do people go to the trouble to build unneeded houses, largely for the sake of exchanging said currency, even when there are dozens of standing, vacant, pleasant houses in multiple decent, pastoral, American neighborhoods right here in Houston, if the currency is, in fact, philosophically worthless?

A plethora of empty houses should bring down the prices of renting and buying residential property. The currency is a tool to make the market work and bring to bear the context of the geography and players that do exist, in fact, in time and space. The currency is not designed to exist at the fiat of property owners, although that seems to be its current and intractable disposition as the homes sit empty while the purported prices of residential occupancy do not budge, or even increases while people are crammed like cordwood into tenements and storage spaces that are close enough to my back door to hit with a football. These circumstances draw into suspicion pricing regulators, property owners, and residential service providers, to name a few agents or institutions. Legally speaking, this house would be a tenement because I do not own it; however in light of the apparent situation at large, I would say that by natural law, no one owns it, and the neighbors own their homes because they occupy them. It certainly begs questions about the landlord and the lease broker.

[*Editor's note: I am curious of the disposition of this property following my move out. The property broker might put someone else in there who will pay in dollars. If not, there is still demand and it will be met, like it is being met throughout the neighborhood. The academic question is, what of such duplicity in a marketplace?*]

So what is causing the hang up? What is retaining the status of the lack of liquidity of the currency in the market? Meanwhile, there are empty houses on one side of us, people living in storage sheds on the other, while the urban sprawl continues to spread at the city's extremities.

As a mindful consumer, I have done everything to audit and monitor the forensics and impact of my household and consumer logistical demand. For example,

I have streamlined, canceled, or switched all utility and service contracts for less polluting and/or less economically costly alternatives. I will not purchase anything non-recycled if there is recycled material available, regardless of price. Such personal marketplace guidelines represent and underwrite my demand for competent logistical support in progressive community engineering regardless of scale. I have ceased consumption of all animal and animal byproducts. Among various other efforts, I count land and air traffic and reckon at the volumes and compositions of their feedstock and exhaust, constantly observing and recording. I maintain a mindfulness of every person I see, every building I see, every oxygen-yielding plant that I see, every animal, anywhere, everywhere, anytime, in order that I will meet no person or thing who is a philosophical stranger. I monitor all construction or land development that I encounter. I try to do everything I can think of and continue to look for additional ways to enfranchise and elucidate my position as a citizen and an operator in a marketplace, in order to identify and mitigate any or all of my intractable demand upon the marketplace, and to some important degree, that of my peers in the market and community as well, in order to strengthen an in-good-faith currency's function as a tool.

It is an effort to narrow the currency down to a representative one-for-one philosophical dollar value of general equity, everywhere as much as possible, at which ratio the currency can best serve as the intellectual tool that it is, rather than serve as a commodity that it is not. One must realize that actual currency is not worth the paper it is printed on, but the idea is that it underwrites diligent market activity in good faith. Yet, with all of the people around here just kind of living where ever, and doing whatever whenever, or collecting cash in-kind from desperate people, or just generally living their lives, I am still required to pass currency, although I am not sure that anyone else is doing anything but gathering it from me, although the economic system is not guaranteeing my retainer through compensation or employment. I am still trying to figure out what information I am missing.

The at-large situation is not being properly managed, if managed at all, and in the company of many, I seem to be the only person who has qualified the situation as headless. Am I the last cop out? Am I entrapped? Is it statutory? If it is, it would seem that the same statute would be a construct of some state whose jurisdiction is currently failing to maintain a normalized, functional, applicable currency and economy, and there would be no legitimacy to any of its statutes. Maybe I am in charge, in fact, and people are just bullshitting me because they know it is true and they know I don't know it.

I say "I" instead of "we," because although I do find a nice "we" at some times and places, and we seem to be doing fairly well with managing our world and creating order and beauty in our community, there are many times and places where there is no "we," only "me" and a bunch of seemingly foreign and rarely handsome strangers. Some of them want me to give them currency, but I typically give out pocket bibles to people who ask me for money, and maybe I should get some pocket Dhammapadas also. Some of them want me to smoke cigarettes and drink alcohol and snort cocaine. Some want rent. Many desire very strongly to have my phone number, or social security number, or credit card number, or address, or name, or any other item of information that would allow them to involve themselves in my origins or my dwellings, or shoot me in the back or hit me in the head with a baseball bat when I'm not looking. I think that some of them might want to eat my brain. These things are known among the

Buddhists as hungry ghosts. On the other hand, rarely does anyone offer me currency. In fact, I have grown effective enough at being an investigator that all corporations do not wish to employ me.

Defining the state as a functional construct comprising the representative electorate and its enfranchised or vested incumbents, there appears to be no agent-apparent of the state in this situation but for me, at times. When there is a functional state order there is no agent to broker a management agreement among the labor force, production, and the service sector but for myself. When there is nobody qualified, I suppose it's just a domain of humanoid insects running around burning the gasoline and drinking the water of the good earth. My firm is incorporated in the state of Texas and has a federal tax number, but the firm is categorically for-profit, even though it does not turn a profit. How does one register one's self as some sort of variable government entity? I suppose one does not, rather it is an application of American constitutional law that is incidental to one's daily business, or by specific contract. Or is it by simply registering to vote, or with the draft board, or by holding a state university degree, or paying sales taxes or income taxes? Am I a cow being raised for food? Am I an ox being raised for labor? We may have a locust problem.

I am trying to put a finger on it. It is almost like the situation is the result of child's play gone awry, and while I seem to feel closer and closer to some revelation and relief on the issue, it is as if the main hook is just someone or something being intentionally troublesome. I have, for years, increasingly prayed and meditated on peace and benevolence and harmony in the world, and I try to spend every living moment being mindful about all living beings, in order that when I see homeless people near the backyard, or under bridges or where ever, there is quite essentially zero effort in leveling these people up as subjects of my holistic mindfulness practice. Because through a ceaseless mindfulness practice, basically, I always will already have taken any stranger ever encountered into account, and so it is just a pro forma matter of spotting and confirming someone on my life's path. In some real sense, my repeated prayers for me and my family, for us to be appropriated to where we are most needed, have been answered here by these people living in a storage shed behind our neighborhood, as well as by my awareness of the apparent large-scale economic fraud and disorder in the community that is occurring in plain view. These prayers and meditation are the driving force behind what dislodged me from my former job which must certainly have been my last cubicle job. But there is still a question of how to proceed, in gentlemanly fashion, and how to allow my requested, sought after, granted, achieved role in the greater spiritual and sociological community to coincide in harmony with the ongoing business maintenance of my family and household.

It seems apparent to me that, basically, the people who are living in the alleys behind me are my, or our, people and my, or our, responsibility in very many philosophically real ways, because I may be the only one who even knows that they are there and who also happens to actually care. If and when I am not here, maybe no one cares. They are added to the class-action prayer, meditation, and mindfulness practice which, as a point of order, I already maintain and have groomed through the years. But this perspective seems to be egregiously taken advantage of, and frequently.

There is also a community center/church-like institutional center, cater-cornered to our property, and although it was not saliently marked with a crux or steeple, there was a significant crowd in the parking lot, playing basketball and such, when we drove through the area, being that it was early Sunday afternoon. There was community leadership apparent, that is, two individuals keeping an apparent general pastoral watch in its parking lot. The nearest standing steeple is north of here about two blocks.

Ruble v. Dollar

August 12, 2013

I have a Russian Federation 1,000 rubles note, which as of yesterday was said to be valued at about $32.80. I searched the listings for nearby currency exchange locations, and the nearest appeared to be a Goldwiser precious metals dealer in the H.E.B. shopping center at the corner of Bunker Hill and Houston's Interstate 10/Katy Freeway westbound.

It was the lunch hour as we arrived at the grocery store's indoor strip mall, and the sign read Texas Gold and Silver Exchange, not Goldwiser, but I tried anyway. The answer was no, the store does not exchange foreign currency for dollars, the young woman said. It smelled kind of like burning cocaine in there, but no surprise, as this odor is not unusual around people who have been smoking crack. I don't know what else to call it but advertisement. Besides me and my son, the only person apparently in the store was the woman behind the desk. Maybe the crack smoker had just left right before we got there.

Maybe a Spanish galleon loaded with the golden spoils of antiquity is expected to sink any minute in the Houston Ship Channel, and such an at-the-ready gold-exchange operation can be thought of as critical infrastructure, I cannot know. Anyway, barring perhaps its forensic value among burglary and theft investigators, I am uncertain of what good is to be served by exchanging gold for fast cash, which is what the store purports to do, and for apparently all the wrong reasons based on the smell. In a vacuum, to pawn gold is to buy into a currency system, in my view, but this particular operation is no good advertisement for whatever currency systems are involved. Maybe I am sentimental, but it is probably not wise for anyone to do business with a financial institution that is conducting an overt prostitution operation with real hookers, or maybe it was a fake prostitution operation in order to conduct narcotics interdiction using real crack smoke as bait.

I am not convinced that this or other similar operations are conducting business in good faith. I would like to see the contracts for the use of that commercial strip. Regardless of what is being used to bind the property's use, the situation potentially presents a problem related to the disposition of rights-of-way in the state of Texas. If operations at the location are ancillary to criminal activity, then I and my market peers have important things to say and do about it. Greater Houston has more than just a squatting problem.

A few doors down in the same strip mall was an International Bank of Commerce (IBC) franchise, so, in light of the store's name, I inquired there as well. The answer was no, the store does not exchange any international currencies for Americanos, but that its franchise location down in Houston's Galleria District does. Incidentally, none of the half-dozen staff, including the young woman who was identified to me as the "bank manager," looked any older than early twenties. It did not smell like crack cocaine in this one, but the people looked sort of surprised that I had come in and asked a question. I was peppered with apologies as I was shooed out of the store. I am not convinced that operation was in good faith either. It certainly is not doing what its name would seem to imply that it does. I had a gut feeling that the location was operating in a similar fashion that I had encountered during a local cell phone franchise location incident which engendered a recent investigation and formal criminal complaint from me—e.g., where the "manager" is an imaginary rich person and everyone involved with the operation is an "assistant manager," and nobody involved can spell "MBA."

Never mind that for all of its grand survival instinct, the fake bank IBC will not provide simple accounting or financial services such as currency exchange. It would be one thing for the conspirators to cheat and steal in the name of a bank if they were actually providing the usual array of accounting services that are expected of bankers, and it certainly would make them less obviously suspicious. I don't think they even know how to pretend to look right. Either that, or they are not even trying.

At this point, we left the building and went back to the vehicle. My son, bless his heart, who is seven years old, has learned to be patient during my frequent, long, awkward conversations with uniformed strangers in public. We stopped again at a nearby Bank of America franchise, located in the same business commercial area at the northwest corner of Bunker Hill and Interstate 10.

The young lady working the door, like it was some sort of bar or restaurant indicated that, yes, the store did exchange foreign currencies for dollars, but only if I had a Bank of America account. I told her that I do not have a Bank of America account, and asked why it was necessary. Such a policy comes across as a vote of no confidence in the currency around which the institution is trying to build a cottage industry.

Again, I question the basic integrity of this operation. The bank had, at the very least, failed to educate its staff regarding the operation's fundamental role in a marketplace. Maybe the bank is broke, and all of the people in there were conducting some sort of other unrelated "business" anyway. I say, just provide me with the service; it would be a friendly thing to do, and would make it appear as if the business is legitimate.

From there, we headed on to the Interstate 10 eastbound feeder road, where a few blocks east of our previous location we stopped at a business called "U.S. Coins." Supposing that it might provide currency exchange services, I parked and went in. The building's security was far more evident than the previous locations. The woman governing the front entrance said the business only bought and sold rare or otherwise collectible money and the like, and that it did not provide accounting or financial services like exchanging foreign currencies for dollars. But, she did suggest that I go in and have one of her men look at the bill. She pressed a few buttons to unlock the pathway to the business area, a room full of glass-encased displays containing various kinds of monetary artifacts including an antique printing press and a multitude of collectible currencies. I explained my task at hand to a gentleman behind the counter, who looked at the bill, and agreed that since it was not very old (printed in 1993) the bill was not really any sort of collectors' item. Notably, I did not detect any outright signs of narcotics use or prostitution at this location, although the gentleman behind the counter had the type of condescending, subtly combative, disagreeable, nearly childlike disposition that is typical of people who are more focused on the fact that they are lethally armed rather than the at-hand dialog. They seemed very certain that I was doing something wrong, but they weren't sure what it was.

A few blocks farther east on the I-10 feeder road, before reaching the intersection of the I-610 loop, I noted a sign that read Goldwiser, which of course was the name of the place I was trying to go in the first place. We stopped and tried the door, but it was locked and the "open" sign was turned off. I had a perfunctory conversation with the proprietor of the locksmith shop next door, who did not know anything about the spooky closed-in-the-middle-of-the-day Goldwiser store, nor did he know a thing about the Harris County Sheriff's Office either.

Two important lessons of the day: 1) Apparently it's OK to point a gun at someone if they don't know it, and 2) Only actual hustlers need to do so.

We left, U-turned, and began driving back toward our neighborhood. At the southeast corner of Blalock and Westview, there is a "Wells Fargo" franchise. I have used Wells Fargo since it bought the institution which housed my checking account back in the late 1990s or early 2000s. I will probably not bank with them for much longer, and I have been phasing out my use of the account, because I believe my affiliation with the institution is scaring off potential business patronage and causing my personal and household accounts to be ill-regarded in the marketplace.

Anyway, I made the last stop of the trip at this Wells Fargo location. The time was about three o'clock, and like the Bank of America, the room was crowded and bustling. I put the question to one of its staff. Yes, she said, the location does exchange foreign currencies for dollars, and she prompted me to go to the teller. The teller asked me what kind of currency it was, as the print on the note is written in Russian Cyrillic, and he evidently did not recognize it. After several minutes of his referencing an international currency identifier handbook, the teller informed me that he would not exchange the bill because there was not an identifying picture of it in the book. I was politely escorted to the door with another volley of apologies and funny looks.

Ad Hoc Constant Flux Electronic Networks

September 28, 2013

Gena Konstantinakos' first independent film takes a satirical angle at the governance and economics of the World Wide Web in the United States of America.

On Sept. 9, the short film documentary *The Internet Must Go* debuted on-line. By Sept. 20, the film had been viewed 144,000 times, the filmmaker said.

Incidental to the Sept. 9 debut, oral arguments were heard at the United States Court of Appeals for The District of Columbia Circuit *(Verizon v. Federal Communications Commission, Case No. 11-11-1014 D.C. Cir. 2014)*, involving litigation by large corporate communications firms petitioning their interests with respect to the Federal Communications Commission's regulatory role regarding Internet traffic, according to *Jurist*, the web-based legal news service published by the University of Pittsburgh School of Law.

The Internet Must Go harshly mocks apparent corporate efforts to transform open-form Web content in the United States into a sort of commercial/pay-television style of programming.

Konstantinakos said that she is not a policy expert, but that the film is intended simply to raise awareness about the subject of domestic Web regulation, and to get more people involved in the conversation.

"For everybody who uses the Internet, this is something they should be paying attention to," she said. "We take for granted that the open Internet is here to stay, but that is not necessarily the case. The term "net neutrality" really means your Internet Service Provider cannot mess around with content and loading speeds. I do not like the ISP telling me what Internet I have access to. It is similar to the water company weighing in on what I am allowed to use my water for."

Accurately Defining Terms

Should not the major ISPs be able to do their bidding in a mutually exclusive manner from the majority community of net users at large? By the very nature of such communications infrastructure, does not the Web's logistical redundancy protect against inept regulatory management or clouded corporate foresight?

As currently categorized for regulation, there are considered to be four main ISP companies in the United States: ATT, Comcast, Time-Warner, and Verizon. However it is worth pointing out that the term "Internet Service Provider" is a misnomer. The Internet is the de facto array or distribution of electronically, non-locally networked client interfaces on the planet at any given time. The scope of "Internet Service" at any given moment varies, and any snapshot of it is determined by the connectivity status of all on-line networking clients at a given instant.

"The Internet," strictly speaking, cannot be "governed" in function or in nature from outside of itself, and is also not monetizable in the traditional sense. It is an ad-hoc network, and it is in constant flux. Our society's extant computer networking technology has advanced to such a powerful, scalable disposition that there is no real need for external micromanagement from the top, at least not as it has been historically understood and implemented. Forensics, yes; incidental infrastructure management, yes; generalists and experts, yes; but the network itself is an unavoidable (albeit wonderful) consequence, or "symptom" if you will, of our technological status. By design, it does not respond to "top down" management.

So, the regulators and the "major ISPs" are not even correctly defining the key parameters of their purported bailiwick (if we are to believe what we are told about the matter currently at hand in the D.C. Circuit court). And in case you have not noticed, the presence of around-the-clock data and connectivity has, within a span a few decades, antiquated all previously extant economic standards and protocols of day-to-day business, just for starters.

Putting the Genie Back in the Bottle

Logician Kurt Gödel argued, in criticism of Whitehead and Russell's *Principia Mathematica*, that "no axiomatic system whatsoever could produce all number-theoretical truths, unless it were an inconsistent system," cognitive science professor Douglas R. Hofstadter wrote in his Pulitzer Prize-winning novel *Gödel, Escher, Bach – An Eternal Golden Braid* (1979). Historically, and even still today, each time the Internet "changes" by even one networked interface (which is constantly occurring), it is a unique manifestation in a series of random parameter models of electronic networking. In real time, the 'Net functions as a working analog of a quantum computer. Each little variance in the ongoing flux contributes to and endless river of macro-configuration snapshots that are crucial stepping stones for the present and future of ever-higher levels and complexities of computation and networking. The constant flux illumines critical pathways to the study and observation of solid state, and, yes, even quantum logic. In case you had not noticed, the Internet is alive and intelligent, just like the planet and the sky, just as does shine anything else that has been dipped into or manifests out of the fertile aether of our cosmos and collective mind.

In the future, I predict that "ISP" will be historically considered to have been "any and all people and organizations who did not understand the basics of electronic networking nor collaborative communities in general," or, "the people and organizations who tried to liquidate, for debtor's note cash, a key aspect of humanity's technological saving grace."

Net Signal, Infrastructure, and the Obligations of Common Carriers

In the United States, regulation of the commonly used, shared communications infrastructure rights of way (rail lines, highways, utility easements, and standard electronic communications thoroughfares such as terrestrial and planetary airspace) and their upkeep are a public asset in any practical sense, because they provide critical services to the constituency, so there is a responsibility of the citizenry and its government, with respect to precedent obligations of common carriers, to maintain clear and functional rights of way, regardless of whether the items being transported are lumber, school children, electricity, or data signals, etc. In the spacious United States of America, such a regulatory ability calls for centralized, compartmentalized bureaucratic clearance to ensure open and functional rights of way (for data, the crucial payload is often first-responder communications traffic, industrial communications networks, and commercial logistics, for examples). Our government agencies can be put upon to regulate the infrastructure and rights-of-way which, among many other things, happen to carry the crisscrossed ant hill that is non-local electronically networked computer data traffic (e.g. "the Internet"). And remember that without us, there is no such agency.

Historically, the "web" data in transit was networked on top of existing telecommunications (common) carrier networks. Apparently, however, the current regulatory disposition determines that broadband cable and so-called digital subscriber line carriers are not common "telecommunications carrier service" providers but rather private "information service," providers. This enables marketing monopoly situations wherein there are no more than two "ISP" options for purchase in a given local geographical area, typically in the form of one cable provider and one DSL provider. This, in essence, cuts a gift cake for a handful of companies that are doing business as the possessors of existing infrastructure and rights-of-way, and provides for them to sell logistical space for data traffic on what is essentially a public asset that would not be possible without the complex, interwoven, highly redundant, highly random electronic network that is extra-local, unrestricted, and un-shunted in terms of its networking parameters. In many ways, "the Internet" is one of the most piecemeal things conceivable; it cannot be possessed by any one person or company, and it cannot be turned on or turned off.

The middle man has been identified and isolated, people, and the culprit is: Whoever is billing you for data service. Technically, they are an unneeded middle man. Some people are aware of this fact, and some people are not, and there appears to be some liars on both sides of the dividing line. Being billed for infrastructure maintenance and infrastructure installation is one thing. Being billed for access to a communications network infrastructure by a company that does nothing more than rent out end-user modems for access to infrastructure whose foundation was installed fifty years ago by some other company before it was busted up for being a monopoly, is not supposed to be the way it works. It is not always that way, but it certainly can be, to varying degrees. Simply because the "major ISPs" spent a lot of money adding a lot of high bandwidth infrastructure in the 1990s in anticipation of profiteering from a digital boom does not mean that they can lay grandfather claim to ownership of all domestic communications rights of way, or rights. They shan't be rubber-stamped or otherwise allowed carte blanche to do so by lawmakers whose sole source of vested authority is that of mine and yours.

Suggested Solutions

One way to solve the issue would be to formally nationalize the ownership of the infrastructure, sort of like the Interstate Highway system is, so that the right advocacy of this critical asset ends up being enforced by ethical motorcyclists rather than wolf men, or men without hats, or coked up business-suit types who would not know a data packet from bird wash. Some type of "nationalization" would be the fundamental management default that best reflects the dynamic geography and nature of the asset as a whole, in my view, in order to keep it up and running. Additionally, the companies that are the day-to-day keepers of the various legacy infrastructure and its historical rights of way provide nice quasi-technical jobs with good benefits for engineers and technicians, but the role could be happily and handily taken over by the U.S. Army's Network Enterprise Technology Command. How's that for streamlining.

Nationalization would also prevent the market content from being determined by the passive, futile, dying whims of the immanent constituency of reality television addicts and the like. This sort of management is why television programming, despite its vast, vast potential, is significantly determined by and squandered by greedy rat-poison dealers and consumed largely by functionally illiterate people. Television can be thought of as "what became of the Earth's Internet the last time someone shunted the network and replaced it with fiscal-revenue-based content management." (If there was a last time; but how would we ever know.)

Another option for monopoly busting would be to properly reset the regulatory definition back to the common carrier status that it correctly had previously (which, is really no different than the nationalization option provided in the previous paragraphs. It should be noted that the erstwhile common carrier situation was ruined by people taking advantage of the system in bad faith). Then, any basement-dwelling hack with the proper phone jack and know-how can function as an ISP in any given community of basement dwellers or funny-hat wearers or hangliding enthusiasts or whatever, which is how it was, until the "major ISP companies" (purportedly; for I was not there although I did hear tell) gamed the regulators, in order to try to turn a technological revolution and historical-bridge moment in the history of humankind into, essentially, pay television. I, for one, am not interested in either pay television (except for *Deadwood*, but it ended) nor regular television, but then again, I am a geek who is too busy working in my basement to mess with that kind of shit.

The ISPs can monopolize that style of programming all day. They can have it. And I and you and whoever else is not interested in consuming it can stick with our backwater of ad hoc networking, for example discussing obscure and boring technical projects with online contacts;

reading peer-reviewed papers about interstellar warp drives, quantum theory, nanotechnology, and biochemistry at Cornell University's arXiv.org; and watching grainy anime streams which for all we know are originating from somewhere deep in outer space and arriving by way of the stars of Orion.

"If there were more providers it would be a different situation, but given that there is a limited choice, then to limit the content would be a very serious thing to do," Konstantinakos said.

"It has been great to observe the comments that are popping up on-line, which anybody can see on Facebook or YouTube," she said. "It speaks to the fact that people do care about this, and it is presented in a format that is more easy to digest. Some are occasionally confused, not understanding that it is intentional satire."

The short film's impressive 144,000 views reflect how open networking and widespread access to a diversity of content through the Internet allows for a free-flowing marketplace of ideas and original thinking, she said.

So, what prevents the net from just remaining what it has become? That is, largely engineered and governed by an ad hoc potpourri of technicians and hackers, academics and amateur enthusiasts, et al? Should not the marketplace simply let the "major ISPs" sell a poorly networked "fast lane" (to nowhere) if they want? The major ISPs can freeze their shares or entirely sever their affiliation with the dollar, and go live under a rock, for all I care. I believe that is the usual prescription for people acting in bad faith when plying the public coin anyway. They could re-run soap opera advertisements in their "fast lane" all day, every day, and they can, for example, try to relegate the DefCon archive and various other technical forums to the "backwaters" of the web. In their eyes, they will have won the day, with their "private virtual networks," which sounds like another name for the type of ad-cluttered, pay-content crap that is available in motel rooms with their feces-covered remote control units.

The general public should have nothing to fear from some ongoing corporate litigation involving people who have no idea what they are talking about. But don't ever forget to vote, just in case. Also eat your vegetables, and if you are not doing yoga, you should start. Anyway, Konstantinakos' film does make an excellent point, that such dangers should be nipped in the bud, and that keeping an eye out for threats like this, whether they are hypothetical or not, is crucial.

Migrant Labor, Community Management, the Dollar, and Over-the-Counter Narcotics

October 23, 2013

Typically we do not eat gas station anything. But recently, while we waited for a tow truck to fetch the family car, I got some trail mix at a Shell station on Interstate 10 near our home.

As we shopped, into the store came a crew of day laborers and their leader who stood and watched as the various men who were covered in dust and paint from the day's work made their selections and lined up for the clerk. We got in line to purchase our snack. A second foreman-looking guy perused bulk-packaged beers in the back of the store.

It appeared that the laborer directly in front of us in line purchased his two tall cans of Budweiser product with U.S. dollars. With the same hands, the clerk brokered the transaction for the liquor he bought, just as promptly and competently as she did for the snacks that we bought.

As the value of the dollar directly correlates with the skills, abilities, and products of the nation's labor force, this foreman is not handling the tool in good faith, and is not properly representing his de facto, ad hoc peers with whom he shares both the marketplace and the currency that represents the vested authority of the citizenry.

Even outside of the currency argument, the foreman's act is not occurring in good faith so there are common moral implications in addition to any constitutional arguments. It also reflects horrific management and policy, comparable to shooting one's horses at the end of the day because the custodian is too lazy or unwilling to feed and stable them. Or, like habitually leaving your tractor in the rain instead of the barn, and buying a different one every time the old one rusts out.

Civilly, these men who apparently do not know any better than to take the blue pill offered by the foreman, are in the foreman's custody and as such they are significantly at his ethical and moral mercy as their temporary employer. And when he does his deed by way of the U.S. dollar, he does it in my and your name, and it is very much our problem.

Thomas Hobbes' *Leviathan*, Part 1, Chapter 16: "When the actor doth anything against the law of nature by command of the author, if he be obliged by former covenant to obey him, not he, but the author breaketh the law of nature; for though the action be against the law of nature, yet it is not his; but contrarily, to refuse to do it is against the law of nature that forbiddeth breach of covenant."

That is, we're contractually bound and responsible. Our vested authority as citizens is a great responsibility. That's the civil liberties argument.

The American dollar functions as a symbol of a particular value as it relates to specific goods or services in a marketplace, while it allows us to avoid the actual use of laborers and artisans as legal tender. It exists as a tool to serve and enable the labor force, and something is critically wrong when a currency does not reflect the heart and objective best interest of its underwritten workers. That's the civil rights argument.

Hobbes' words contextualize how the foreman, when using the currency to provide beverages containing ethanol to adult human day laborers who appear not to have the cognitive wherewithal to avoid addictive and deadly over-the-counter narcotics, is creating, among many other hazards in the community, an extremely precarious moral and ethical liability for us. The common law firmly places the moral liability upon us. Per Hobbes, the foreman's error is primarily significant because of the liability for a violation of law that is placed upon the author (the citizens) of the currency (the public coin of our evidently abundant common wealth) *stare decisis.*

Specific rules of labor and immigration aside, the sanctioned open solicitation of day laborers is relatively common in Houston because the city is of significant enough distance from the Southwestern border that the chilling effect of immigrations enforcement is not as strong as it is for such labor pools in border cities, for example. However, even then, the city of Houston has other pick-up locations besides beer stores (such as underneath the Westpark Tollway, for example, between Beltway 8 and Highway 59). To wit, if the contractor wants to exercise civil disobedience, his beer-store method is nevertheless morally inferior to his Westpark Tollway option. By his methods, he is creating additional demand for this undesirable way of doing business, moreover he is using the public equity to do so. He is eroding the currency, damaging the free market, assaulting the labor force, taking away from the common good-standing of the community, and mocking the system of public government and its constituents.

This activity shows blatant disregard for human welfare and the overall health of the people. The drunk man has to go somewhere, and the sun must also rise on his body at some presumably nearby location in the morning, since he probably walked to the convenience store where I observed him parting ways with his employer. Evidently, the foreman does not care if the man returns to an ad hoc day labor pick-up location the next morning, or even whether or not any of the men live or die, or he would likely demonstrate his care by orchestrating the situation differently. Maybe the men do not care either, as there must still be, or at least there used to be plenty of people besides day laborers who do this to themselves intentionally every day after work, but that is no excuse.

The laborer may not need any additional encouragement from the foreman who is enabling his alcohol abuse, through which eventually he will become unemployable, and then what? Where is the foreman when first responders, public health facilities, welfare programs and the like must bear the burden for the demise of entire socio-economic generations of people, to which these historical unethical "business" practices contribute? Is the foreman presuming to be held harmless because he gave them the currency and watched them make the transaction, rather than having physically bought it for them himself?

Who trucked the liquor into this neighborhood anyway? I did not order it, and neither did I nor anyone in my family order any drunk people. Come to think of it, I do not know anyone who did. Perhaps the foreman would not be so quick to dump off his liquor-enabled laborers at the end of the day if he were releasing them into his own neighborhood. A 'live and let die' motto is not as attractive when one makes the mess in his own house.

City of Houston namesake Sam Houston was a United States Army General, and John Richardson Harris (Harris County namesake) was from New York but he was a businessman and a marine merchant; and I expect that they would both have something philosophical to say about the foolishness of intentionally destroying employable laborers. Furthermore, I expect they would concur that alcohol among the ranks is unquestionably known to be poison in the well of power or complex systems or anything else; as such, when it is intentionally administered, it is administered in bad faith and/or ignorance, and always negligence.

As members of the same ad hoc marketplace consortium whose labor, products, and services, in addition to our vested authority as citizens, are represented by the common currency, we are put upon to intercede operations such as these from misrepresenting the fundamental civil will.

Support of this type of ethically deviant labor practice by soliciting or patronizing it, regardless of how widespread it may or may not be, is unacceptable because it perpetuates the behavior and feeds the hazardous subculture underpinning it. Simply because a behavior or habit may be "culturally accepted" (whatever that means), or because it is commonplace (or rare) in a given community or context, does not make it necessarily ethical or right behavior. Typically this sort of activity occurs in open broad daylight, because people are either simply unaware of what they are witnessing, or because people think there is nothing that can be done about it.

There are times when doing the right thing simply means not to do the obvious wrong thing. Labor management, with no exceptions made for shift leaders, is obligated and duly compelled to be ethical in the United States. Exercising such ethical responsibility in business enables different cultures and people to learn to get along and build community bonds. This breaks down the walls that prevent natural communication and open markets in all thoroughfares, including the interface between labor and "labor management," and allows egalitarian government and ethical marketplaces to function properly.

Proposed Legislation Prior to the Second Session of Arizona's 51st Legislature

January 2, 2014

Arizona's 51st Legislature will reconvene on January 13, with a number of interesting bills proposed. At this time, there are thirty-five Senate Bills and sixteen House Bills pending review.

Of the early-posted senate bills all but one were put forth by Democratic lawmakers. Of the house bills, fifteen were put forth by Republicans with the other one being a bi-partisan effort. For whatever reason, most bills do not crop up until the session is under way. The up-to-date list of proposed legislation can be viewed at www.azleg.gov. The state lawmakers can be sorted out at www.ballotpedia.org.

Lobbying, Public Officials, and Disclosure

Senate Bill 1034 proposes amendments to the Arizona Revised Statute regarding public officers and lobbying, and its presence alone on the docket begs questions about what was occurring that compelled the author to pen specific rules restricting unethical behavior in public office where, minimum thresholds of quality and common goals toward level-headed lawmaking should already be demanded and expected in good faith.

In addition to other statements and reports already required by law, SB 1034 proposes that, as a matter of public record every public officer shall annually file with the secretary of state a verified financial disclosure statement with specific dollar amounts covering the preceding calendar year. Such disclosure would cover any benefit received by the public officer or her household members or relatives to the second degree of consanguinity, if the benefit is in the form of travel, lodging, or registration fees related to a conference, meeting, or other event, regardless of whether it is denominated as a scholarship, a reduced rate, or full or partial reimbursement. The required descriptions would itemize the benefit received in the form of travel, lodging, and registration, and disclose the name and address of the donor or payer of each benefit, with no minimum amounts.

SB 1034 is proposed by Democratic District 9 Senator Steve Farley of the Senate Ethics, Finance, Government and Environment, and Transportation Committees.

New language regarding exceptions to the registration rules of lobbyists is also included, and notwithstanding those, the bill puts forth that a person who engages in lobbying as defined in the ARS must comply with the registration and reporting requirements.

Ethical Marketplace Operations of Residential Mortgage Brokers

Another follow-the-money-related Senate Bill is 1026, and as with the lobbying/public officer bill, it seems to have been put forth to shore up unethical behavior. This one is in the realm of banking and real estate rather than public office and lawmaking, but in either situation, the abuses of the system would involve misappropriation of the American dollar, which in itself is a public contract representing the vested civil authority of the citizenry, and is thus everyone's business.

SB 1026 puts forth amendments to rules for

residential mortgage brokers with stipulations that such brokers shall not make, provide or arrange a residential mortgage loan without verifying the borrower's reasonable ability to successfully budget it. It would also forbid "churning" (knowingly facilitating a residential mortgage loan if it does not provide a reasonable, tangible net benefit to the borrower under the circumstances at hand), and would forbid facilitation of a mortgage loan with the intent for it not to be repaid but rather for the broker to ultimately obtain the title through foreclosure. SB 1026 also would forbid facilitation of a residential mortgage loan that is of a lower investment grade than allowed by the borrower's credit score without first informing and getting written consent from the borrower.

The bill would also preclude direct and indirect coercion or intimidation of an appraiser for the purpose of influencing independent judgment about real estate either involved in a residential mortgage or that is being offered as a security on a mortgage application. The other stuff denotes fraud and ought to be common sense in the marketplace, but this last one should certainly already be covered by criminal statute, so I suppose there must be some cause for tort reform.

Again, one might expect that piecemeal reform would be unnecessary, since our jurists are sworn to uphold the American constitutional law which affirms the civil liberties of the citizenry that includes, for example, people's natural rights not to be robbed by mortgage brokers. No judge in this land needs specialized legislation to apply the law of the land. The presence of these proposals draws into question the competence of the state courts, or perhaps their administration.

SB 1026 is put forth by District 26 Democratic Senator Ed Ableser, of the Senate Commerce, Energy, Military, Public Safety, and Transportation Committees.

State Education Department

The Senate's current pre-gavel docket also includes several education-related proposals and amendments. Ableser's Senate Bill 1016 proposes that all public school personnel must receive at least two hours of suicide awareness and prevention training beginning with the 2015-2016 school year.

Senate Bill 1029 would provide for the department of education to fund adult education and adult literacy programs from state tax revenue. Specifically, the revenue would comprise all state transaction privilege tax, and all use tax from retail sales of various oil and gas transport and storage hardware. Revenue would also come from gross proceeds of sales or gross income derived from any contract with real property owners for the maintenance, repair, and replacement of existing property (this would exclude modification activities). The system would be implemented at the end of December 2014.

SB 1029 is put forth by District 9 Democratic Senator Steve Farley of the Senate Ethics, Finance, Government and Environment, and Transportation Committees

Nutrition

Ableser's Senate Bill 1018 would require, by July 2015, the department of education to develop nutrition standards for high schools that are separate from the ones set forth for elementary schools, middle schools, and junior highs.

"The nutrition standards for high schools shall meet at least federal guidelines and regulations for foods and beverages sold on school grounds of schools that offer instruction in grades nine through twelve during the normal school day. These nutrition standards may include guidelines regarding portion sizes appropriate for high school pupils, minimum nutrient values, and a listing of contents. This subsection does not prohibit the department from developing minimum nutrition standards that are more stringent than the federal guidelines and regulations for foods and beverages sold or served on school grounds during the normal school day [sic]."

It is good news that lawmakers are attempting to effect change in this matter, because diet is critical, particularly in the context of academic systems (not to mention the unavoidable correlations between diet and health and thus healthcare systems). The fact that the language does not prohibit the department from moving to more stringent standards than the minimum threshold federal guidelines is good news too, because the minimum federal guidelines are grossly insufficient, as exampled by additional language in the same proposed bill:

"Schools that offer instruction in grades nine through twelve shall provide a variety of beverage choices to high school pupils, such as bottled water, juice drinks that contain 100 percent fruit or vegetable juice, isotonic drinks and low-fat milk. Not more than 50 percent of the available beverages may include diet and unsweetened teas, zero-calorie carbonated drinks, sports drinks or juice drinks that contain less than fifty percent fruit or vegetable juice."

That means one-half of it can be crap.

"Beginning July 15, 2015, new contracts and renewal contracts for food or beverages, or both, shall limit the selection of all diet and unsweetened teas, zero-calorie carbonated beverages, isotonic drinks or juice drinks that contain less than 50 percent fruit or vegetable juice to not more than 50 percent of vending machine capacity located on the campuses of schools that offer instruction in grades nine through 12. All other foods of minimal nutritional value shall be expressly prohibited on the campuses of schools that offer instruction in grades nine through twelve during the normal school day."

Nutrition scientists and athletic coaches will insist that carbonated beverages and diet drinks are "poison" and completely useless at best, and vending machines full of it (or half full of it) do not belong on high school campuses, or really anywhere, at all, ever. It is difficult enough for many young adults to make crucial important decisions, while facing all kinds of negative solicitations and misinformation, even without the sanctioned availability of garbage for food from their custodial institutions.

On another nutrition note, Ableser's Senate Bill 1019 proposes that chain restaurants or food establishments must properly analyze food and beverages for nutritional content, and clearly and conspicuously list the total number of calories, trans fat, saturated fat, carbohydrates, and sodium for each food or beverage item on the menu. It also would provide for compliance inspectors and penalties for non-compliance. It might be appropriate to add one more sentence to SB 1019, something like, "nobody should eat fast food, because it is of questionable origins, and is not good for you, and if you prepare your own meals, it is healthier and far less costly to the consumer and to the marketplace."

[Editor's hint: One's diet determines whether you will live or die]

Solar School Program Fund

Farley's Senate Bill 1030 would prescribe and enforce policies and procedures to install solar technology in public schools, and establish a fund for net metering at each school using solar technology.

Solar School Fund Program revenues would be transferred to the maintenance and operation section of the budget, and the governing board would distribute money received to the school districts for the installation of solar technology in new and existing school facilities with priority given to smaller schools.

The bill also establishes a new tax that would begin at the end of 2014, comprising 0.05 of one cent per kilowatt hour of electricity delivered to residential customers, 0.07 of one cent per kilowatt hour of electricity delivered to commercial customers, and 0.07 of one cent per kilowatt hour delivered to industrial customers (excluding any kilowatt hour that is generated from renewable sources).

[Editor's hint: Solar panels are a key part of humanity's survival on this earth]

Exploratory Committees

Ableser's Senate Bill 1025 would establish an individualized education program study committee. The committee would have four certified teachers who are members of a statewide teacher's labor union, four charter school teachers, two public school administrators, and one member who is involved with a statewide partnership devoted to education reform and innovation.

The committee would select a chairperson and design a system through which an individualized education program is developed for every pupil enrolled in a public school. The committee would be given purview to request information, data, and reports from any state agency or political subdivision of this state; hold hearings, conduct fact-finding tours, and take testimony from witnesses including participants in the educational system. On the request of the study committee, a state agency and a school district or a charter school shall provide to the committee its services, equipment, documents, personnel, and facilities.

The department of education and the state board for charter schools would provide staff and support services to the committee, which would be required to submit a report of its findings and recommendations to the governor, house, senate, and secretary of state by the end of December 2014.

Ableser's Senate Bill 1028 would appropriate $40,000,000 from the state general fund for fiscal year 2014-2015 to the department of education for distribution to schools that have been assigned a performance letter grade of D or F, for the purpose of rehabilitating the performance of these schools.

Ableser's Senate Bill 1027 would establish a Phoenix Sky Harbor International Airport Study Committee, whose membership would comprise two members of the senate from different political parties, two members of the house from different parties, and three members of the public.

The committee would elect a chairperson and study the future of the airport to include its ability to expand and service a larger metropolitan area, as well as study the feasibility of having additional airports to relieve air and road traffic at Sky Harbor International. This committee would also study the economic impact of expanding the airport and regional hubs with respect to such issues as access, efficiency, and availability to commercial interests and the flying public. The committee would submit a report of its findings and recommendations to the governor, the senate, and the house by November 2016.

Homicide Quid Pro Quo Arizona

March 1, 2014

During the 51st Arizona Legislature, there have been proposed several bills related to capital punishment, but only one of them (which involves tacit re-enforcement of existing capital punishment policy) has made it through committee review.

In 1972, the United States Supreme Court ruled in *Furman v. Georgia (408 U.S. 1972)* that the death penalty was tantamount to cruel and unusual punishment therefore it is in violation of the Constitution. However, four years after the Furman ruling, the court made a more nuanced ruling in *Gregg v. Georgia (428 U.S. 153 1976)*, holding that capital punishment was not cruel and unusual under all circumstances.

With these precedents in mind, Arizona House Bill 2680 would have established a capital punishment study group to assess whether capital punishment in Arizona is administered in a rational, fair, and accurate manner. However, HB 2680 was never assigned to committee for review by Speaker of the Arizona House of Representatives Andy Tobin, according to Dan Peitzmeyer, president of Death Penalty Alternatives for Arizona.

There are hundreds of bills proposed during each legislative session, and many of them do not make it to committee, presumably because there is simply far more legislation than the assembly can handle. However, it is unclear what criteria determine which bills are reviewed for potential enactment, and which are not. Regarding another unrelated bill that was not assigned to committee by House Speaker Tobin, Sen. Debbie McCune Davis said in January the criteria for such procedural decisions are political and not objective. There is no law being violated when a bill is ignored and not placed before legislative committee, but it is an administrative failure that effectively suppresses the voice of the equal constituencies which are all represented by all legislators regardless of any partisan affiliation, McCune said.

Another piece of legislation in the current session, Senate Bill 1067, proposed to repeal the death penalty by statutory amendment. This would have replaced capital punishment as the most heavy-handed criminal sentence in the state with imprisonment for natural life without parole. It was put forth by Senators Ed Ableser, David Bradley, Steve Gallardo, Katie Hobbs, Robert Meza, and Representative Juan Mendez. The bill went no further than the Senate Judiciary Committee as the committee Chairman, Sen. Rick Murphy, district 21, declined to hear it, Peitzmeyer said.

As went SB 1067, so went its companion legislation, Senate Concurrent Resolution 1002. SCR 1002 sought to amend Article II and Article XXII of the Arizona Constitution, adding the language "no person shall be sentenced to death in this state." This resolution was proposed by the same lawmakers as SB 1067.

From another angle of the issue, House Bill 2313 proposes to add smuggling, human smuggling, and a probability of violent recidivism to the list of aggravating factors which are available for consideration by death penalty prosecutors. The bill was put forth by Representative Justin Pierce, and unlike the anti-capital punishment legislation proposed during the current session, HB 2313 seems to be moving right along. Pierce's bill was heard before the Senate Judicial Committee on Feb. 13 and in the Senate Rules Committee on Feb. 18. It had a second reading in the senate on Feb. 27.

Habeas Corpus

In instances where a government entity breaches its purview of control over individuals, the issue arguably becomes an affair of state and no longer is strictly a problem of executive enforcement and administration of bureaucracy.

The habeas corpus protocol that originated among the English common law, today has analogs in many nations. Consideration of capital punishment begs ethical questions related to state jurisdiction with respect to people's actual selves and arguably about people's souls as well. In the United States, a writ of habeas corpus has the power of a court order and can be brought to test the context and validity of a prisoner's detention; the writ's purpose is to protect against unlawful detention (that is, any detention that is based on insufficient cause or evidence).

There should be some historical category of prisoners who have served their entire natural life in prison because their wardens successfully showed sufficient cause and evidence for their detention at a habeas hearing. Arguably, however, regardless of any disposition of guilt in a capital case, the concept of habeas corpus is still legally relevant when defining the limits and scope of the state's power over an individual. To wit, the state may argue to keep the prisoner for his or her entire natural life, but whether or not the state has the moral right to dispatch the soul by inflicting physical death is an entirely different conversation.

So, does a state have the right to kill its citizens?

"I don't think so. I think it's barbaric to think the state can kill its own citizens," Peitzmeyer said. "The state is us, and we are fallible human beings, and we make mistakes. I perceive taking life to be fundamentally wrong. Evil people need to be separated, but we can protect society without taking lives."

The Arizona Attorney General's Office is the agency responsible for prosecuting capital cases as well as all state felony cases. Typically, in seeking some administrative perspective when considering this topic, one might expect all questions to be directed at the Attorney General.

The issue remains legally compelling outside of the bailiwick of Arizona prosecutors and any others who might be expected to similarly follow the letter of the law in prosecuting capital crimes. In the interest of habeas cases in the context of the greater global or international community, or in a moral context, and because it is a fundamental truth that capital punishment could be wrong policy, a question regarding the broader or final liability of capital punishment seems to be overdue.

So, in a democratic system, who is ultimately liable for the death penalty? In whose name is it occurring? In addition to the Arizona Attorney General's Office, a question about the public's potential liability was put to both the Arizona Secretary of State and the United States Secretary of State. Neither directly answered the question.

Question: "What can a person or a group among the Arizona constituency do in order to avoid potential exposure to liability occurring as a result of the public contracts (i.e. the dollar, public office) being brought to bear in "statutorily legal" homicides in the state?

Arizona Secretary of State: "Thanks for your inquiry, but in Arizona the Secretary of State serves chiefly as the Chief Elections Officer," said Matthew Roberts, the Arizona Secretary of State Office communications director. "We also have a business services division where we process notaries and charitable organizations, so we don't have anything to do with this sort of thing."

U.S. Secretary of State: "Your query would be best answered by the U.S. Department of Justice at (202) 514-2007. Additional contact information can be found at (the website). Thank you for contacting the U.S. Department of State."

So, if you are held incommunicado in Arizona, and/or without cause, and/or without being informed as to why, perhaps you might try seeking relief through the British Consulate. Or, run for state office. Meanwhile, the stated federal advice here was to contact federal prosecutors, which is probably good advice, as the DOJ appears to be on the up-and-up during the current administration and has not yet hauled me off for asking honest questions.

In his response to the same question, the chief of capital litigation for the Arizona Attorney General's Office took a narrow perspective, citing the letter of the law as the ultimate source of procedural wherewithal in his vocational purview. His response, however, still left unanswered the question of who, in a democratic system, is ultimately answerable to the consequences of the existing capital punishment laws. (The answer in terms of common law and more specifically U.S. constitutional law is "all citizens," and that answer is legally binding.)

"For this office, we are tasked with defending state sentences and convictions, whether it is a capital offense or not," said Jeffrey Zick, chief counsel of the Capital Litigation Section. "You put aside any personal feelings, because you're a lawyer and, if you practice in Arizona, you defend the Arizona Constitution and the United States Constitution."

Arizona Case Law

A good Arizona example of progressive yet sufficient sentencing as an alternative to capital punishment was arguably made in the case of Jared Loughner. Loughner pled guilty to nineteen federal charges of murder and attempted murder after a shooting spree in 2011 in Tucson that killed six people, including a chief U.S. District Court Judge and a 9-year-old girl. Thirteen other people were also injured in the attack, including a member of the Congressional delegation.

The federal charges and sentencing of Loughner were accepted by the surviving victims as sufficiently severe and Pima County elected not to sentence the killer under the state's effective capital punishment laws, Peitzmeyer said. Loughner is currently serving seven life sentences plus 140 years at the U.S. Medical Center for Federal Prisoners in Springfield, Missouri.

At this time, there are no scheduled executions in Arizona, although there are 121 inmates on death row in the state. Of those currently on Arizona's death row, four have exhausted their appeals options.

According to the Arizona Department of Corrections, the agency that operates the state prison system, the most recent execution in Arizona was Robert Jones, on October 23, 2013. *[editor's update: Joseph R. Wood III was executed on July 23, 2014 at the Arizona State Prison Complex in Florence]*

The conviction and sentencing of Jones and his accomplice Scott Nordstrom stemmed from two deadly armed robberies in 1996. On May 30th, the two men entered the Moon Smoke Shop in Tucson, where Jones immediately executed a customer with a gunshot to the back of the head. One employee escaped and two others behind the counter were shot at by Jones (one suffered a non-lethal bullet wound and the other was missed by the shot.) A fourth employee was executed by Nordstrom with two shots to the head. Money was taken from the store and shared with the lookout David Nordstrom.

Fourteen days later, Jones and Nordstrom entered the Firefighters Union Hall in Tucson; three customers were executed with gunshots to the head by Jones. The bartender was shot dead by Nordstrom after failing to successfully open a safe.

Oral and ethical prudence and legal culpability in all capital cases is not always as seemingly clear as it appears to have been in the Jones case. Philosophical opposition to capital punishment as a general practice includes arguments regarding the availability of competent and fair legal representation for defendants, and concerns about evident arbitrariness and lack of parity in the implementation of prosecution policy. Other questions include complexities about the mental fitness or competence of defendants to stand trial and understand the gravity of their crimes; and historical instances of inaccurate determinations of guilt or innocence. Since the death penalty was reinstated in the United States in 1973, there have been 143 people exonerated of capital convictions, by being acquitted of all charges related to the crime that placed them on death row, or by having all charges related to the crime that placed them on death row dismissed by the prosecution, or by having been granted a complete pardon based on evidence of innocence.

In 2002, Ray Krone was released from Arizona's death row after DNA testing exonerated him from his 1992 murder conviction and death sentence. His conviction was said to have been based mainly on circumstantial and forensically tenuous bite-mark evidence. The first film in a collection of documentaries, *One for Ten*, which tells the stories of innocent people on death row in the United States, features Krone's story.

Krone will speak at the Arizona Summit Law School, Room 1737, 1 N. Central Ave., Phoenix, at noon on March 7.

In 2013, the U.S. Supreme Court ruled in *Trevino v. Thaler* that death row inmates in Texas can initiate claims of ineffective legal counsel in a federal court if they did not have a meaningful chance to do so during state appeals. In the Texas case, the court applied precedent from its ruling in *Martinez v. Ryan* in 2012. *Martinez v. Ryan* had provided such a right in an Arizona case where, according to the Death Penalty Information Center, Arizona state law otherwise forbids raising such a claim in a defendant's direct appeal.

Another Arizona case, which has been cited as an example of arbitrariness in capital prosecution, stemmed from a 2002 homicide case in Phoenix. Defendants Patrick Bearup, Sean Gaines, Jessica Nelson, and Jeremy Johnson were accused in the ball-bat beating and shooting of Nelson's cohabitant Mark Mathes, whom Nelson suspected of stealing $600. All but one defendant secured plea bargains and avoided trial. These three included the person who instigated the crime, the person who beat Mathes, and the person who shot him. Of those three, according to the DPIC two of them will probably be released within fifteen years.

Bearup was the only one of the co-defendants who received the death penalty, although he is said to have been not directly involved in killing the victim. By the prosecution's legal theory, he did not cause the physical death of Mathes, rather the extent of Bearup's involvement was cutting off Mathes' finger to take a ring, and assisting in disposing of the body.

"Throughout our country, there is nothing uniform and throughout our state there is nothing uniform in the application of capital punishment," Peitzmeyer said. "We are executing the poorest and the least educated in the state. Here in Arizona, it is essentially only applied in Maricopa and Pima counties because they are the only ones who can afford to do it. It is not a deterrent, and cops on the street will tell you it is the smallest tool in the shed."

The capricious dollar also seems to have a role in determining for whom and in what jurisdictions prosecutors seek the death penalty. The *New York Times* reported in April 2013 that Mohave County deputy attorney Greg McPhillips, citing budget restraints, had documented that the northwestern Arizona county could only afford to try one death penalty case at a time. For this reason, McPhillips had reported that his office had elected not to pursue a capital case against a man charged with first degree murder, child abuse, and sexual assault of his infant son, instead pursuing the death penalty for a man accused of killing a teen and injuring her mother.

Says Peitzmeyer, it is far cheaper, in terms of dollars, to house someone for a lifetime than to execute them. And in light of budget trouble which has led the state of Arizona to sell the capitol building and legislative complex which it now leases back from their new owners, the cutting of costs through the repeal of Arizona's death penalty is a sound argument for several reasons, he argues. Also, states without capital punishment have lower recidivism rates, he said, which also presents a savings to any community.

This year, on January 8th, the U.S. Supreme Court

rejected indefinite delays in federal review of capital cases where inmates are not mentally competent to assist their attorneys. The opinion, written by Justice Clarence Thomas, cited the rear-looking, record-based nature of most federal habeas proceedings that allows attorneys to identify legal errors and build arguments without client assistance. This opinion from the high court consolidated two cases: Arizona's *Ryan v. Gonzales (568 U.S. 2013)* and Ohio's *Tibbals v. Carter (218 U.S. 2012)*.

If a death row inmate is mentally incompetent, he may not be put to death, according to the Supreme Court's ruling in *Ford v. Wainwright (477 U.S. 1986)*.

However, the January 8 opinion reads, "Where there is no reasonable hope of competence, a stay is inappropriate and merely frustrates the state's attempts to defend its presumptively valid judgment."

Ironically, the court's disposition seems not to address the apparent bureaucratic no-man's land or blind alley between federal protections and state rules, of the sort which the high court sought to remove in its *Trevino v. Thaler (189 U.S. 2013)* disposition.

So who says capital punishment is wrong, and why?

Quite simply, the answer seems be a religious one, and probably political, too. For example, Peitzmeyer's first response was a reference to the "thou shalt not kill" clause found in the Decalogue.

"Execution is contrary to most of the world's religions. I find it abhorrent," Peitzmeyer said. "Killing people to show that killing people is wrong does not make any sense. It is cruel and unusual punishment and in violation of the Eighth Amendment of the United States Constitution. It is arbitrary and capricious."

"The death penalty is about punishment, not

rehabilitation," he said. "And in the thirty-eight years since it was reinstated, we have come to realize that we can't get it right."

Not Alright For Fighting: The Pet Shops Plug Electric in Phoenix on Friday Night

April 17, 2014

England's synthpop/New Wave group Pet Shop Boys will be in Phoenix on Friday night in support of the band's latest (twelfth) studio album release *Electric*.

I remember the band's hit "West End Girls" playing in full rotation on MTV in 1986; I was in middle school and I think I was technically still an innocent. We drove to the nearest big city (Houston) to see the Pet Shop Boys play circa 1991, by which time I was a full-blown teenager and had become far less innocent in the eyes of local secular authorities.

When I listened back at that song this week, I was flooded with an azure nostalgia, of the sixth grade, and then of the twelfth grade. And when I listened to the copy of *Electric* provided to me by the group's press agent last week, although the music did not have the extra depth of being twenty years gone, I still found it to be stylistically true-to-form enough with the band's historical body of work as to touch upon that same pond of nostalgia.

The band's perspective is still peaceful and frank, and its artistic illustration of the world and society is done with a detached, cool, effective perspective. The music is, still, full of hooks but not riffs, so it's catchy, but also pacifying, and there is no hangover or unintentional reverb. No accidents.

The album's first song, "Axis," introduces a fresh, faithful, successful effort at the type of orderly and rewarding electronic dance music which is, in terms of its being appropriate for headphones, just as aesthetically and technologically important as any high fidelity 1970s album rock. So *Electric* is redeemable in terms of its application as a piece of sleek visual audio.

The album's second song, "Bolshy," has the musicians planting the seed to clone themselves, or reinforce their crops, or as you like it, in the minds of the band's fan base who might find peace, security, and quarter among some comfortable, detached, neo-communist intellectual geography.

The introduction of the album's third song, "Love Is A Bourgeois Construct" (which somehow for me evokes up images of bored sociology students wearing sunglasses at night), salutes the aesthetic of the glistening black vinyl of Eastern European pop rock that was ubiquitous in the early 1980s. The piece also deploys a repetitive rhetoric which serves as a sort of meta-nonfiction. It urges the attentive listener away from traditional pre-apocalyptic values and toward a hive mentality and its safety in numbers for way-finding and for exploration for such things as kinsmanship, romance, or adventure.

"Fluorescent" is an upbeat standard club mix with minor angles and shifts and it reflects the dance club scene from the era of the band's birth. Further, the songs lyric's deliver a sublime cautionary tale that one might hear from any wise and well-tenured survivor of any decade's nightclub scene, or maybe from a narcotics officer.

Both "Inside A Dream" and "The Last To Die" deliver the group's classic trademark style and sound that is cool and detached but still rich with color, recorded with broad strokes on a lush, paint-by-synthesizer audioscape.

All of the mixes on this album are very danceable, although "Shouting in the Evening" is a notable pulsing throbber, and its winding up, shifting gears, and climaxing several times makes for a great club piece. Dancing is good exercise, people.

"Thursday" features accompanying vocalist Example and is another of the tracks on this LP that hits home with the band's legacy trademark style.

The last track, "Vocal," might be interpreted as a self-portrait of the band with respect to their simple wisdom of self-awareness as audiophiles and the band members' ongoing role as a cohesive artistic vessel.

The group shows a commendable ability to whip up their unique sound and style in a refreshing and palatable incarnation, as well as a welcome willingness to keep on bringing it back across the Atlantic, and to the U.S. Desert Southwest.

The show is at Comerica Theater, 400 W. Washington Street, 9 p.m.

Debating the United States Constitution

May 9, 2014

With the August 26 Arizona primary election quickly approaching, the state's summer will soon not just be an oven, but an oven that will spawn a slew of political hot potatoes.

With that in mind, and in the spirit of community dialog and public discourse, former Maricopa County Prosecutor Shane Krauser, and perennial democratic candidate for Arizona's U.S. District 4, Mikel Weisser, participated in the Freedom's Fight Night Great Constitutional Debate event Tuesday at Poston Butte High School in San Tan Valley. The event was put together by Krauser's American Academy for Constitutional Education of which he is the founder and director.

The friendly contest was in a modified Lincoln-Douglas debate style, comprised of argument based on four questions. The event was sponsored by the Conservative Business League, and another is scheduled for May 13 at Casa Grande Middle School.

As the evening's conversation centered on the interpretation of a primary historical source document, it seemed to place Weisser in a naturally weak rhetorical position. Krauser's position brings a more rigid interpretation of the Constitution's language.

Generally, as a "Constitutionalist," Krauser argued in conformance with his stated political platform, which centers on the axiomatic moral or philosophical simplicity of the United States Constitution. Debating and defending this point of view is generally an exercise in defending a very semantically and philosophically defensible position.

Meanwhile, Weisser defended his known democratic-minded platform. In contrast with Krauser's sharp, simple and historically interpreted position regarding the founding fathers' consensus, Weisser's approach to government is philosophically rooted in respecting the founding fathers while also understanding historical shades of gray and societal change.

The program comprised four questions.

Question One: Should there be no limits on the exercise of religion?

Krauser quoted the First Amendment, which reads "Congress shall make no law respecting an establishment of religion, or prohibiting the free exercise thereof; or abridging the freedom of speech, or of the press; or the right of the people peaceably to assemble, and to petition the Government for a redress of grievances."

"Congress shall make no law...," Krauser said. "The converse (or opposite) of that is that the government cannot take sanctions against an individual because of their world view. Problems arise when we tell other people what to do. There is a constant attack on the free exercise of religion."

Krauser cited the recently failed Arizona Senate Bill 1062, sometimes referred to as "the denial of service bill," which was vetoed by Governor Janice Brewer during the second session of the 51st Arizona Legislature. It was one of several pieces of model legislation encountered among various American state legislatures to allow individuals to refuse service based on religion. Some media dialog reported SB 1062 as discriminatory of homosexual, bisexual, or other non-traditional gender dispositions, although Arizona law provides no express protection against discrimination on the basis of sexual orientation. SB 1062 would have enabled a blanket application of denial of service for religious reasons.

"The fact of the matter is, we really shouldn't have needed a law like this," Krauser said. "A person does not lose their faith because they start a business, a person does not leave their faith at the door."

And regarding the question of no limits on freedom of religion, Weisser said, "that is an abstract statement and when it comes to reality, there has to be a limit. We have to have reasonable expectations of what is appropriate and what is not."

Weisser posed to Krauser the hypothetical question of whether, if done in the name of religion, killing babies would be protected as religious freedom, to which Krauser responded in the negative and the men agreed.

"It could be said that America's history has been our attempts to live up to the founding father's ideas," Weisser said. He pointed out that the original English colonies on this continent were established either in the name of religion or in flight from religious persecution.

"The bottom line is that just because a person is free to do something does not mean it has value," Krauser said. He suggested it is better to use market forces to discourage unwanted behavior.

On the other hand, "freedom from religion is under attack," Weisser said. "And market forces do not solve issues of criminality or morality. Our constitution was made to protect us from having other people's religion forced upon us."

Question Two: Is the Constitution a 'Living, Breathing' Document?

"Yes, from its conception," Weisser said. "It is written to continue to adapt."

Weisser cited any number of negative historical sociological aspects of the era of the founding fathers, such as racism and sexism, as arguments of why the Constitution must be viewed as a flexible document that must be interpreted in its respective contemporary context.

Krauser's answer to the question: "There is no such thing."

A Constitutionalist perspective holds that the basic structure of government and the United States Bill of Rights (the first twelve constitutional amendments) is an effort at underwriting and protecting true axiomatic liberty, no more and no less.

However, even with that perspective, these documents were as potentially prone to misinterpretation in the late 18th century as they are today, but that can be said to represent a failure in interpretation, not necessarily a failure in the spirit of the documents, which are fairly straightforward, semantically.

"The Constitution basically states that men and women are born free and men and women with power cannot be trusted," Krauser said. "It's meaning is not altered," he said. Krauser questioned the soundness of a political foundation that "evolves with time," and he warned that such ongoing adjustment and "constructionism" lays the foundation for "the tyranny of the majority."

In addition to changes in social enlightenment that

have occurred, Weisser questioned the wisdom of such interpretative rigidity in light of changing technology, which he said the forefathers were not able to anticipate in the late 18th century. For example, what would have been the founding fathers' intent regarding Fourth Amendment protections against search and seizures in a modern technological context?

Krauser suggested that the simple truth of the Constitution and the Bill of Rights can be preserved, without constructionism or derivative interpretations, through allowing the more complex roles of government to be taken on by the individual states. He reiterated that the Constitution was engineered to provide the most simple and effective protocol for the federal government, in a political environment that was extremely wary of strong central governments.

Weisser said that constitutional amendments generally reflect subsequent changes which are "all reflections of the society at the time."

Question Three: Should the General Welfare Clause be Limited?

Article 1, Section 8 of the Constitution stipulates powers of taxation for the U.S. Legislature, for the purposes of paying the debts of, and providing for the common defense and general welfare of the United States. Varying interpretations of the term "general welfare" tend to have implications regarding the size and role of the federal government.

"We live in a system of government that is simply too big," Krauser said. "The bigger a government is, the less free people ultimately are."

Appropriating for the general welfare of the nation is

not meant to be a catch-all phrase of everything barring neglect, Krauser said. Broad interpretations of the general welfare clause lead to incorporation of federal roles that lead to an oversized bureaucracy. Such an interpretation is also not consistent with the inclinations of the founding fathers nor with historical precedent.

If the general welfare clause were intended to be all-encompassing, Krauser argued, then there would be no need for the iterations in Article 1, Section 8, such as the postal road and army/navy clauses.

"There's nothing about food stamps, there's nothing about healthcare at the federal level, because those are best left to the states," Krauser said.

"I do not understand the idea of rejecting a government because it is big," Weisser said. "That's OK. We have a country of 300 million people; we have a country that covers a continent. Why would we want to limit what we do to promote the general welfare? Stop looking for some excuse to use the Constitution to stop caring about the rights and the lives of others."

Weisser said the general welfare clause is not limited to the stipulations subsequently named in Article 1, Section 8, but rather is a phrase that provides moral direction regarding what can be appropriated by the Congress.

"If we are not looking at the general welfare of all people, even ones that we don't like, then we fall into the trap of special interests," Weisser said.

Question Four: Should the Second Amendment be Altered?

It is only twenty-seven words: "A well regulated

Militia, being necessary to the security of a free State, the right of the people to keep and bear Arms, shall not be infringed."

On its face, the meaning of the sentence seems to be that of a clear and unambiguous instruction for orderliness among the militia, regardless of whether said militia is a proxy of a homeowners association or that of a fleet of merchant marines, in the context of an ad hoc system where individual self-governance and autonomous local governance are responsibilities put entirely upon the vested citizenry.

Weisser's initial response: "Not really, but it should be enforced. I believe the Second Amendment gives us the guidelines of what they were expecting to get out of a militia."

However, a "big obsession with guns, or the worship of guns, which are a tool for destruction," is problematic, Weisser said. Weisser also said that he is a pacifist but that he does own firearms, and clarified that neither he nor the local Democratic caucus has a platform of taking away guns or gun rights.

Weisser said the U.S. Bureau of Alcohol, Tobacco, and Firearms' existing limitations on firearms are appropriate.

Krauser labeled Weisser's position as a type of "Utopian Pacifist," noting that he would also label himself as such, technically. Krauser took a position that the ATF is an illegitimate agency, inasmuch as its establishment occurs beyond the purview of Congress stipulated in Article 1 Section 8.

"I don't know why we live in a country that constantly divides itself over someone's right to have weapons," Weisser said.

Channeling the Authors of the United States Constitution

May 17, 2014

Discussing the intent of the authors of the United States Constitution has become all of the rage since the turn of the millennium. One of the foremost supporters of the constitutionalist movement in Arizona, the Goldwater Institute, hosted attorney and author Timothy Sandefur of the Cato Institute earlier this week.

The event was one of a handful of public events put on by the Goldwater Institute each year. The organization describes its function as an "Arizona-based conservative public-policy, advocacy, and research organization."

Besides his work at the Cato Institute, Sandefur is also the principal attorney at the Pacific Legal Foundation. Sandefur heads up the foundation's Economic Liberty Project, which, according to the group, "protects entrepreneurs against intrusive government regulation." He has written articles for numerous magazines and newspapers as well as appeared at news outlets, primarily Fox News.

Rights and Privileges

Sandefur related a story to the group about 17th century political philosopher John Milton, whose *Doctrine and Discipline of Divorce* was controversial. The doctrine resulted in an investigation by the British Parliament as to why the author had not sought government permission to publish the tract.

The story was part of his explanation of the legal concept of "prior restraint" which derives from English common law. In contemporary American context, the term is used in connection with dialog about free speech.

In the 17th century, there was a sea change with the application of prior restraint, as Whig intellectuals put forth the idea of "rights as rights" rather than "rights as privileges." Such a philosophy of law was part of the foundation for the American Revolution, Sandefur said.

Prior restraint denotes a "permission society," as opposed to a "free society, where, essentially, the government had to ask you to do things," Sandefur said. A constitutionalist or libertarian rhetorical position typically holds that such a "free society" frames the intentions of the "founding fathers" of the United States of America.

"Freedom means not having to ask permission," Sandefur said. "If you have to ask permission, you are not free. If you do not have to ask permission, you are free, but you have responsibilities."

The country's founding fathers took the precedent against prior restraint yet further, with the concept of religious freedom, such as in George Mason's *Virginia Declaration of Rights*, and in Thomas Jefferson's *Virginia Statute of Religious Freedom* which were precursors for the First Amendment's establishment clause and free exercise clause in the United States Bill of Rights. These documents put forth the concept of "liberty" rather than "toleration" for religious practices.

The idea of a society of permissions being replaced by a prescription for freedom can also be observed in the establishment of early for-profit business corporations in the United States. In the early 19th century, these corporations were called "self-organized societies," Sandefur said. In 1819, the United States Supreme Court recognized the first private for-profit corporations that were not a branch of the government.

The speaker said Milton's experience with the prior restraint investigation compelled Milton to write *Areopagitica*, which argues against the rule of prior restraint, and in favor of rights to freedom of speech and expression. This tract also established principles that form the basis for modern justifications for freedom of the press.

The Birth of the Progressive Era

The "Progressive era" which began in the late 19th and early 20th century undid much of the libertarian implementations of the founding fathers, Sandefur said. Supreme Court cases he cited as examples were *Muller v. Oregon (208 U.S. 412 1908), Adkins v. Children's Hospital (261 U.S. 525 1932), Buck v. Bell (274 U.S. 200 1927), and, Abrams v. United States (250 U.S. 616 1919)* which is an important source of today's free speech jurisprudence.

Rather out of step with its contemporaneous Progressive era, the Supreme Court's *Adkins v. Children's Hospital (261 U.S. 525 1923)* ruling is still reviled by the judicial and legislative elite, Sandefur said. The decision set a precedent that federal minimum wage legislation for women was an unconstitutional infringement of liberty of contract as protected by the due process clause of the Fifth Amendment. The interpretation purports that such a threshold wage destabilizes the job marketplace and erodes the labor force's ability to negotiate contracts. This interpretation also suggests that a minimum wage creates a non-egalitarian environment among the labor force and the economy at large.

This must be why there is a federal minimum wage in place today, that is not considered to be a living wage. In the spirit of the Adkins ruling, the federal minimum wage is the sort of result that can be expected by a party who is unable to negotiate any tractable labor contract.

A "Progressive" philosophy holds that rights and privileges are given by a government for the government's own purposes, or as Justice Louis Brandeis put it, "rights of property and the liberty of the individual must be remolded, from time to time, to meet the changing needs of society," Sandefur noted.

Such Progressivism cab easily be viewed as a classist position.

The Progressive era, which Sandefur said is in many real ways still at hand, can be thought of as a period where democratic process takes precedence over libertarian ideals of freedom, although he pointed out that the word democracy never appears in the Constitution nor in the Declaration of Independence.

I would editorialize here that "democracy" is a method or political system, that originated in the classical period of Ancient Greece, and it means "rule by the people" (as opposed to "rule by the elite"). Both have been around for a long time. What's important for you and me today is that we are able to rule ourselves, which at an individual level would be "libertarianism," and among a plurality of self-governing citizens would be "republicanism."

Republicanism could be thought of as libertarianism at a local government or institutional level, sort of like a right to assemble at the state level. Article Four of the Constitution guarantees every state in the union a republican form of government, but that sword cuts both ways, for example if you have incompetent leadership at the state level. There are also hazards with respect to classist philosophy among federal officials, such as which Sandefur cautions against.

So, there is a dynamic of opposing legal philosophies potentially in play, where a progressive judiciary holds that "government exists to make society nice to live in," compared to the libertarian consensus of the founding fathers that the government's role is primarily to protect individual rights, he said.

Progressivism connotes such legalistic parameters of a society where a government gives privileges and permissions through prior restraint, the concept of a "living Constitution," and the concept of "judicial restraint" wherein judges hesitate to strike down laws unless they are obviously unconstitutional.

Judicial Restraint

Supreme Court case examples regarding the concept of judicial restraint given by Sandefur on Thursday included *Kelo v. City of New London (545 U.S. 469 2005)*, which upheld the use of eminent domain by the city and a private developer to take real property away from a private property holder; *Plessy v. Ferguson (163 U.S. 537 1896)*, which upheld state laws requiring racial segregation in public facilities under the separate-but-equal doctrine; and *Buck v. Bell (274 U.S. 200 1927)* in which the court ruled that a Virginia law permitting compulsory sterilization of the unfit (for the protection and health of the state) did not violate the Due Process Clause of the Fourteenth Amendment.

The theory of judicial restraint is exemplified by the practice of "rational basis review." Rational basis review is the lowest of three levels of applied scrutiny used when courts consider questions of constitutionality, whereby only the most flagrant laws, which are not rationally related to a legitimate government interest (which in the United States is the interest of the vested citizenry) are overturned.

"The rational basis test presumes against freedom," Sandefur said.

Arguably, having a society of permissions rather than one of individual freedom carries with it the danger that is sometimes referred to as the "tyranny of the majority" or of "special interests." Therewith, Sandefur angled criticism at Associate United States Supreme Court Justice Antonin Scalia.

"Justice Scalia does not believe in individual freedom, but has said majority rules always," and using that logic, "Justice Scalia has said if the public votes for abortion then it's OK."

"As we move further into a permissions society, we move further away from the blessings of liberty," Sandefur said.

For example, the idea that "money is speech," which modern Supreme Court case law entertains, can be thought of as anachronistic or counterintuitive. However, in an arguably ongoing Progressive era, property rights and rights to free speech can get upside down enough that the suggestion that money is speech does not shock the conscience. I would editorialize here that money represents the elective political will of the citizenry through its vested executive powers of civil agency that is guaranteed in the vesting clauses of the Constitution. Also, the dollar can be used for private debts but it is the common coin of the realm and as such, it is a public contract.

"Money is not speech, money is property, but of

course the government has neutered our property rights so much that we now talk about money as speech," Sandefur said.

As opposed to a progressive approach, such a "libertarian" view comprises a common law reliance on litigation if something goes wrong, Sandefur said, while also putting upon the free man or free woman a fundamental rule to not harm others. A system of prior restraint in which one must receive all permissions from the government, however, "presumes against freedom, which means that it restricts innovation," he said. "And it gives power to people to restrict their own competition."

It also presents a knowledge (e.g. the nuances of specialization) problem, in that "bureaucrats don't know what you should do with your property," he said.

In the Marketplace

Progressivism also poses the problem of permissions or privilege regulators who are not operating in good faith, he said, citing as an example licensing rules at the state level. He noted that occupational licensing is a protocol that is often used against would-be competitors by established operators to prevent competition, although such rules are supposed to be used to prove competency and involve only content related to the particular trade.

He also gave an example of the early progressive-era Supreme Court precedent set by the case of *Dent v. West Virginia (129 U.S. 114 1889)*, in which the court upheld a state law requiring an array of specific medical credentials, and did not recognize Dent's degree from an institution in Ohio. Dent's group accepted and taught the conventional medical science of the time, except that it campaigned against excess drugging and bleeding.

"The legal profession is in the same position today that the medical profession would be in if it determined that health is not its mission," Sandefur said.

Granted, there does sometimes appear to be buffoonery afoot in the marketplace of ideas when it comes to interpretations of the law. But there is a certain semantic recursiveness which represents a nuanced complexity involved in philosophical discourse and applications of law and legalism. The speaker exemplified this subjectivity to his lunchtime audience by posing the rhetorical question of "how do you prove a right to liberty?"

"Rights" can be defined in a conversation, however there is a certain perception of self-evidence that is required to simply understand or experience "rights as rights." That is, "all rights are rights to privacy," Sandefur said.

Many in the United States today have lost the fundamental vocabulary of natural rights and freedom, he said, of terms such as due process of law, public use, and privileges and immunities.

He said the key to resolution of the problem is through education. "Really, there is no substitute for it, for teaching these principles."

He noted the ancient caveats made by the Greek philosopher Aristotle in his *Nicomachean Ethics*, which considered the challenge in communities where the laws are not good and parents must attempt, on their own, to create the right educational environment for young people, without the help from lawmakers.

In broader terms, the classical work by Aristotle discussed the failure of such ethical theory if its aim is not achieved in any applied sense.

Contemplative Forensics 2007–2013

These are excerpts from my personal journal, which has been growing since about the turn of the present century, serving as my ever-boiling writer's cauldron. Barring spot reporting and on-the-fly deadline writing, my journaling has been the springboard for substantially everything I have published. It works as the starter for a variety of content types including fiction, religious essays, political discourse, meditation and dream observations, editorial articles, letters, poetry, and songs.

This section contains several essays of a philosophical shade. In many ways it is a kind of grandstanding; a stretching out and waving of a noodle that is always thinking. Some of these essays are windy and flowery, and some have a bit of an edge. A lot of the content in this section is, for example, particle physics as mangled by a sawed-off newspaper reporter. However, any quackery herein is nevertheless occurring in good faith and is only come by in all honesty by the professed laity. Enjoy.

~CGB, 28 July 2014

Signature

2007

As a youth I was guided along a science and engineering track, but I chose to take the long way home and finished college with a liberal arts degree. Judging by the bullying that is regularly meted out to me by my Linux file server, I suspect that I would have become a software developer. I have managed to establish a toehold in the study of metaphysics where philosophy and science overlap *sic itur ad astra*.

When crossing the street, the territory is the territory unless otherwise noted. In applied metaphysics, the map is the territory thus it is more so important to remember one's place. Metaphysics is a key to free will, and objects of mass are a critical aspect of its imposition. Successful efforts at metaphysical theory require that a distinction is maintained between the conceptual world and the world of objects, as well as knowing the appropriate circumstances and methods by which to suspend the distinction. A working knowledge of metaphysics truly is the key to spoon bending, so to speak.

A navigator and a fisherman may have very different empirical relationships with the same piece of ice. The complexity necessary for evaluation varies with one's relationship to an object and the task at hand.

Visualize in the mind's eye, or on paper, a geometrical construct such as a prism, occurring in the context of a field represented by a sphere. Superimpose the sphere among an additional field or fields represented by additional spheres. Then consider the relationship of the overall array to a field that is not linearly correlated, represented by a cube on a separate sheet of paper.

In the sense that the spheres are entirely subject to the

whims of the experimenter, who may correlate all variables in the model as needed, no relationships among the shapes and their fields are ruled out. Such a perspective can circumvent the observational bias or streetlight effect, wherein the ontological streetlight remains completely disregarded. And as is deduction, it is a means by which to avoid imposing or being restricted by the observer effect.

A fresh approach to issues of modeling and scale avails where one field's sphere is another's dimensionless point, and such things do occur in nature. Through its subjectivity, the model escapes the gravitational confines of Einsteinian relativity. If one's mathematics won't let you force the issue, that's a semantical problem. An empirical description is only useful insofar as it is applicable, and there is an analog of this rule in jurisprudence, that is a contract is unenforceable where it does not conform to the realities of the geography and limitations of the marketplace and its agents. The tool is not antiquated but human agency is compelled to make an executive election regarding the spirit of its application, notwithstanding jokes about the capriciousness of applied metaphysics.

The exercise shows the importance of context in matters of practical philosophical relevance. The map becomes the territory through the application of one's free will. One can experiment with such a living epistemology anytime. One must remain honest in such endeavors. Ethics remains intact. There is no "let's don't and say we did," where some deviation from empiricism does not fit the experience. The discoveries are plenty when investigating the world to see what rules are legitimate, which ones are not, and which ones were always wrong.

Anything can be engineered, theoretically, and any

design implementation is typically built to account for extant or anticipated physical laws. But the local physics are not the philosophical cause of the engineering design, no more than the engineering design is the cause of the physical laws. The cause of the phenomena which the laws describe, is philosophical. In this sense, the notion that engineering design can be the cause of physical laws is in better conformance with the teleology of a living epistemology or a free will than with the alternative notion that the law of the sea or local physics has the causality. In terms of philosophical causality, physical phenomena such as matter and mass are all of a lesser order. Interaction among massive objects may describe cause and effect, but it is not the root of it.

Alternatively, when keeping such a philosophical order in mind, phenomena that may have been previously mistaken as incidental or consequential can be found instead to be a true function of original signature import and meaning. What previously were misinterpreted to be effective ontologically, are instead revealed to be limited to the stuff of objects and calculation.

Vantage

2008

There are parallaxes in writing. The subjectivity of the author's vantage is clear as I compile my journal, when excerpts best fit reversed from the order in which they were written, and I ended up adding fresh copy to the front end of the drafts. It is interesting that my pen travels toward the front of the book, as the pagination goes a different way. The calendar is on yet another track. Come press time, the copy is bent back into its original order.

In a similar way, as I've been reading Roger Zelazny's *Amber Chronicles* to my son, I'm struck that I am occupying the author's personal time line. That in itself is not far fetched, and it probably helps that this makes for my third reading of the series. Wherein exactly isn't clear to me, but I am undoubtedly on the man's time. Regardless of what the clock or calendar or anyone else has to say about his civil disposition, for all practical purposes his body of work is not late.

It follows that beyond any terminus of this flesh, I can remain metaphysically quick through my art and writing. Then and now, and in the worlds of other writers, and among our readership. This is one way to define the muse, in fact. We see that she pays well. So an author can accept that he can come full circle to meet himself, and on his own terms by way of his own mastery.

As scriveners we face our creative parallaxes, which overlap with those of the other guilds. My father was a knife maker, for example. As my back pages stack up, they provide me with ever-fresh perspectives about the nature of the written word, and life, or lives, in general. Just as growth in wisdom over the years incrementally adds room after room of head space among one's house of memory.

Literature becomes infinitely prismatic when exposed to an audience, as the readers provide bottomless potential through their perspectives among themselves and the authors. The potential has proven to be vast.

Mister Sandman

2008
Night School

Friends and I were sitting at an old wooden table on the shaded second story porch deck of a coffee shop. It was a nice day, but disrupting this balmy setting was a screen door behind my chair that swung out and hit the wall with a loud crack, then another sharp report as it slammed back to. I did not turn around to look toward the noise, because my gaze was caught by the shocked expression on the face of my associate who was sitting across from me. He had a better view of the racket's source.

Soon there was no need for me to turn around, as the man who had exploded through the door entered my view as he ran screaming, in a breaking, high-pitched voice, "stop calling me an asshole!" The scream sounded more like an enraged child or injured animal than an adult human. It had the shredding, violent quality of someone who might be suffering a massive crush injury.

It was clear that he was not stopping. One blink later, in a dead heat sprint, that dude encountered the belly-high, second-story porch wall. He didn't stutter-step or even hurdle it. Instead, quick as the wind, he simply straightened his legs backward and bent forward his head, and went over that wall head first. Whoosh. No do-overs. Consequently he hit the pavement downstairs with a fruit-like thump. My partner and I sat in a silent moment.

"Did that guy just…?" I put the unnecessary question, as time stood still.

"Yep," my friend answered unnecessarily, still looking toward the porch wall.

The fauna hit the concrete with a low, dark, and fleshy racket, and then a final vocalization shot back over the deck fence. The witnesses were all suddenly quite alert, and awash in the feeling of innocent guilt that is experienced by unscathed near-miss survivors.

The man's raging declaration of "stop calling me an asshole" had the same cold signature as the bloody cry from the pavement. His brain tardily received a one hundred percent body trauma signal down there, and the throat emitted that alarm when he was already scientifically gone. At that point, the noise was a simple byproduct of his flesh. It was interesting.

I know it sounds cliché, but during the silent, stunned moments that followed the violent suicide, I woke up.

The dream was a weird one and somehow very close to heart. Whatever the content may be, dreams don't lie. Regardless of any specific messages communicated, it was a psychologically explicit study of a human life at the moment of a human death, that was presented to me as matter of factly as if it had been chalked up in a blackboard diagram for classroom discussion.

Daydreaming

Another type of dream are the kinds that occur when you are not asleep. I recall the images impressed upon me when I was a boy, during travels to my grandparents' house. On the five-hour drive, through farm country I would be thinking of my grandmother. In my mind's eye, I would see surreal automaton farm equipment that was even larger than any of the gigantic real-life mining machines I later have encountered as an adult. Daydreams of rusty, massive, skeletonic crop balers. Filling whole mindscapes with their shearing, thrashing, and baling of the endless crop, planetfuls of it, and making quick work of the infinite task. No edifice, only huge, artificially intelligent, metal insects and their feedstock. There was no one operating the anthropomorphic equipment, no people period. Just crops forever, and the sky-high machines, and infinite time. The amber crops and rust colored bones of the crawling, towering, sprawling, par-sentient combines were not the same color, but their various shades of tan also seemed infinite.

Here is a second example of dream imagery among waking life that made it into my dream journal:

"I dreamt last week about a wispy, flame-like tree stump, walking about neck high. I was not asleep, though. It was one of those twilit wanderings near sleep's borders, or sometimes happening in wide wakefulness when the light and the air is right.

The stump was moving about in my physical field of vision, though I had a heightened awareness regarding its relative position with respect to other objects among my surroundings, that made its movement appear subtly geometric and slightly electrifying. On a less subjective level, the stump was smiling a sharp grin. A trickster, a forest sprite or so, but warm and genuine hearted, about the shadows of my apartment and the courtyard below."

Repeat

Recurring dreams involve resistance to applications of natural lucid dreaming techniques, and are symptoms of the mind's working at some trap, puzzle, or challenge encountered in life's walk. Two such dreams from my early childhood come to mind.

The oldest recurring one was always set in the darkest of all nights, among the labyrinthine catacombs and dusty, dizzying heights of a nameless, woods-cloaked manor in an ancient and neverending forest. Thereabout dwelt two bipedal canines, one in blue overalls and one in white. One of them always abetted my flight from the violent and dogged pursuit of the other. Their roles alternated, regularly switching with me caught in the breach. Because the switching never stopped, I could never find lasting peace of mind. Often both of them would be within my view when the switch took place, and I would have to cut and run while I was still breathless from my previous flight.

Inevitably, I was devoured by one of them if not both, if not during one night's round, then whenever the game continued the next night. Caught and thrilled into either waking, or placed back into the cycle as if I were a participant in a live-action video game. I was startled awake while being eaten by a monster animal, or gobbled up only then to find myself replaced in some empty wing of the castle or some obscure leg of the forest. This went on round and around through the nights, and when I was very small, it was every night.

The other dream occurred less frequently, but it continued further into adulthood. As its recurrence diminished in frequency, the last one was more than ten years ago. It also involved a foot race, but this time I was trying to escape from an evil tornado. Sometimes the weather event chased me through houses, or while I was driving highways, or on foot in open fields. And like the overall-clad wolves, usually the twisters succeeded in running down their quarry, either catching up and waking me, or wrapping me up in death.

The lessons taken from these dreams can be as useful as any earned while awake. In my daily business, I have never seen a live tornado, yet from my dreams I am intimately familiar with the unmistakable locomotive sound of a funnel cloud, and I have experienced the thrills of being chased and being carried away by them.

Miracle Valley

2008

Last year, I had an assignment on a Saturday afternoon to cover an old fashioned tent revival, near the Mexican border in southeast Arizona. It was another dusty, sunny, and windy day on the high desert grassland. I filed the piece with the managing editor, but that evening while sitting in my apartment, I tapped out a broader angle on my manual typewriter:

"I parked the Jeep and walked toward a suspiciously innocent scene of Americana, befitting a setting from the *X-Files*.

The first man I talked with was a character jumping ship to these pages from *Ulysses*. A gentlemanly octogenarian in a greenish, grayish, dark-brownish wool sport coat and green shirt. He wore a driving cap. He had a dialectical accent and no teeth, so I had to bend my ear way over and squint my eyes to understand him. We talked as we walked to the tent and stood in the rear behind most of the arm-waving congregation.

He said he'd been the on-call chaplain at the county jail for decades. This man, this old stone road through the hills, he was the real story. Gray, slight, but his eyes were bottomless and they became more endless and electric blue with prolonged contact. Doors into a never-ending seaside thunderstorm, swelling behind the words of a great, dark book.

The congregation told of the region's population, containing youth, motorcyclists, army veterans, and young families. A representative sum of the sociological crossroads at hand in light of the military installation to the north, the old mines to the east, the Republic of

Mexico to the south, and mountains all around on the horizon. Ten minutes later, the chaplain offered to walk me to the dining hall to interview the campus administrators.

Representing the sponsoring institution were three men who I interviewed together. The executive administrator was a barrel-chested man who had the stripes of a thought-to-be-extinct species of twentieth century door-to-door or used-car salesmen, a curious man happily swimming up the post-modern bilge from late antiquity. For about eight years, he had been in charge of this campus, and had overseen the implementation of its new assisted living center, he said. We walked through there, and the walls of the main hall were lined with organs, solid-state and tube electrics, end to end.

"You can't take 'em with you," he said.

The head, his two men, the chaplain, and I sat in the cafe around a table for the interview. The quietly busy co-ed students-slash-kitchen staff glanced from the wings, cooking and sweeping. The head talked of the success of the assisted living operation, and later showed me the refurbished building which will become a daycare center by next summer.

The head said he was from the state of Ohio, which supports my theory that all people who claim to be from Ohio are actually aliens who are entirely made out of people-shaped cheese. I don't remember where the second guy said he was from, and the man with the thousand-yard stare did not say where he was from either, but he did wear slick pointy boots, and was one of the institution's original alumnus. He was the most free with his speech about the many miracles he had seen and still sees. He said he expected that we would all be privy to some good miracles on this day. In retrospect, I realize he is right.

Every day is a miracle full of miracles.

It was hard to tell which of the guys' eyes constantly went back-and-forth the fastest, except for the miracle man. His were steely blue, binocular, and unmoving.

They offered water, I accepted. I have drunk out of that aquifer for four years. Still, I have never drunk actual charismatic tent revival water, as far as I know. They poured it for me into a short polystyrene cup. It was cold, mineral-flavored well water. The kind of "hard" water that will yellow one's teeth, over the years, but also makes them very strong. I downed it at once. It was refreshing. The climate is very dry out here.

They showed me an old black-and-white film of a traveling preacher, recorded in the institution's heyday back in the 1960s. The footage captured the man laying hands on a young African-American girl. She stood from her wheelchair as her mother looked on, in the domed worship building that today looks beyond repair.

Those students pushing brooms in the cafeteria came and went from the kitchen. Somewhere in the middle of it, the head put a small audio recorder on the table in front of me, propped it toward me, and I just plowed ahead with my questions and note taking, being long-accustomed to people behaving unusually around reporters. With the recorder on, one of the kitchen co-eds fired up a vacuum cleaner and worked on the carpet behind me for about ten minutes.

After the interview, I toured the vast and dilapidated gathering hall. Its stairs led upward and inward to a huge sky-lit dome. The three leaders talked about coming up with the cash to overhaul it, but it looks pretty far gone, structurally. A woman finished up a prayer in the dome, and made here way back down the stairs."

Standard Branding

2008

After I had been in college for twice as long as most undergraduate programs are intended to last, I chose a journalism major. This is how I can get a toehold on a writing career, I thought. Relatively clean living was enabling me to think straight by that time, but a science degree was still not in the cards. It would have required a great deal of leveling coursework, and that was time prohibitive at such a late hour in my undergraduate career.

I had potential, as we all do, but I wasn't made. Some sweat equity was needed. In pursuit of it, among the various jobs I have had since college, I realized that employers or managers use the term "writer" loosely, to suit their purposes, if not mine. On the other hand, some managers who are managing actual writers avoid the term outright.

The path has been a study in any number of subjects to include emergency response, criminal procedure, global corporate relations, small business administration, sociology, local politics, applied technology, and research and development. The lesson learned is to remember in all circumstances to be careful with labels.

Such duplicity in terms may suit a manager but not the spirit of the marketplace, where it can result in a good-cop-bad-cop dynamic among operators or individuals. One man's ink-stained scrivener is another man's wide-eyed UFO investigator, or one person's over-aggressive marketing agent is another's patsy for institutional fraud. The lesson learned is that labels matter.

Spot

Be at peace.

Breathe

The tea is hot, and wet, but it, too, is empty.

The smell, the taste, the temperature, is not the tea. So, what is the tea?

And what then is the experience. Are the tea and the experience separate?

And if, but for the experience, the tea is empty, is the tea nothing more than the experience?

Does not the experience itself, the interaction with mind, define the tea entirely?

And is not the experience just that – only the experience and nothing more?

The experience is apart from the tea, then? The experience, therefore, is empty?

Does the experience exist? does the tea exist? did the tea occur?

Is the tea?

Are you?

Did it only occur in mind. Where is mind.

In the tongue?

Where else.

Be at peace.

Placid water.

Rain.

Breath

Fertile Crescent

2008

The influence of the starry heavens is heightened in my daily meditation sittings as I spend more time at amateur astronomy.

It is through the cool cover of night time that ocular vision is best directed toward the skies, and the inner eye of the mind also regards the glittering cosmos most clearly through a subtle veil. The need to make use of such shades stems from the grandiosity of the vista, and there is no denying its brilliance.

Ordering these two complementary perspectives shows that neither of them should be considered apart from the other. They are of the same holistic consideration of what I describe as an endless universal vertebrae submerged, in a sandy beach as big as the sky. It occupies some era so distant that the actual fauna is fully plowed under in physical space and time. At such a distance, its reckoning requires metaphysical or abstract perspective to truly visit, but it is true. The effort is accomplished through the cultivation of the mind's eye.

The structure vibrates in the heart through my own vertebrae-rooted cognitive platform. The frequency is common to the bodies, shells, trunks, fibers, stamens, thoraces, pools, and depths of all the fleshy coils, appendages, and crystal caves of my global cohabitants.

As long ago or as far from now as necessary to accommodate the range in the order of measure, from a pristine beach on an antedated sun system, a transcendental organism is broadcasting on all frequencies. Bathed time out of mind in rich starlight, the contents of that beachscape are, in essence, that of infinite generations upon generations of stars, galaxies, and clusters, *ad infinitum* all temporal directions. It is an ontological primordial beach. There's no litter. In some areas the electromagnetic radiation fluctuates, in others its light remains steady. Substantially the material at sea level is ripe, cooling stellar entrails freshly regurgitated from the cosmic womb.

In the surf, nerve-and-bone chains churn among the waves and the tides. The prevalent mode of self awareness ranges from refractive biological consciousnesses to collective latency of the fundamental construct. In the bonds of the silicon, sand, and water, cooling energy overflows from rocky balls swinging about gushing, plasmatic baby suns strung up in a warm place. There is no time but for to glow and grow.

The presence is prominent and part of the secret of its majesty is ubiquity, but it can be overlooked by way of missing the forest for the trees. It reached out and touched my consciousness, and has yours. There is comfort in knowing that we have been here before and will be here again. That is communicated by the presence of this cosmic womb of some ancestor, some sibling, some progeny. A good neighbor.

Time Underwater

2008

With all of the glowing blackness and glistening gravity of an ink jet in an ocean trench, a memory percolated up through my neural net about two years ago, and seated itself in my parlor with the air of an attractive, mysterious package come hoisted up a dumbwaiter. Like a black pearl that no one will ever see, after a decades-long immersion among the petals and corals of my memory banks, it was an especially shiny object.

I and my folks and some kids from our neighborhood were camping at Lake Somerville. After dark, we children walked down the beach to the marina where we were playing on the fishing piers. The water was placid, and the southeast Texas summer night air was humid, still, and clear. When looking into the water, over the railings or through the boards of the interconnecting piers, the water's surface indicated a bottomlessness matching the sky's. The dark plane of the lake surface reflected the depth of the cosmic ocean above and its shower of starlight that constantly kisses everything. Our bodies resonated with the relatively low-pressure, wet, and ionized atmosphere down by the water, and with the ambient weather from billions of miles above also.

Some aspects of the memory seem to have emerged perfectly preserved in a write-protected format, but the relic has gained something during its thirty years in the vault. It has returned alive. It has soul.

The preserved account takes its place among the absolute bottomless infinity of other such memories of all times past. A savory gem hidden in some sheltering crevice forever, among the rich terrestrial lakes and swirling cosmic oceans. A shard of life shaped to quickness by having motionlessly traveled an immeasurable distance in accordance with the sort of time that passes at the bottoms of lakes, while being polished slick by thirty solar years of transport aboard a human memory. Rivers work similar magic.

Natural Alchemy

2009

I have a contemplative streak, egged on by the gnostic gospel of the Christ from early on, and further evaluated through a Buddhist insight meditation practice that I began about the time I finished college. I have kept a meditation journal as well as a dream journal, and as you can imagine, I like to talk as well as write about spirituality, religion, theosophy, metaphysics, and philosophy.

Several summers ago, I was writing a zen tea meditation, considering the world in relation to myself, and scribbling notes in my journal. I realized that the contents of the list I was making were similar to the concept of the "classical elements." Here is the journal entry:

"When exploring inner space, one has to start somewhere, and since the map is the territory when looking inward, anywhere will do to begin. All such efforts must be made with a good foot forward, or right action. Because we are the true sources of spirit and illumination, everything beyond soul and self remains relatively undefined or unrefined, inasmuch as it is irrelevant to one's own philosophical will and presence.

From beyond antiquity, people have explored their worlds and kept written records of it, in seeking minds who are more or less alike to their own, and whose personalities and lifestyles are driven after a like fashion. Perhaps one wishes to find others who want to hunt for buffalo, so she draws a buffalo on the side of the mountain, advertising her disposition. The point is that I am not the first person to use symbols and writing, obviously. And I am not the first person who, during the course of his meditation and philosophical scrivenings, has arrived, by way of my own unique path, at some of the same enlightened perspectives as have various of my predecessors.

It is an important accomplishment when one can make a written contribution, and can satisfy one's own curiosity and contribute to the at-large epistemology, for example with respect to metaphysics and Presocratic dissertation. My incidental, if not accidental, arrival at a valuable subjective observation of the classical elements illustrates that there are certain common rights of way for thought and the mind, and reflects certain shared goals and common ground for enlightenment guided by free will regarding being, observation, and truth. The ability to make such observations *a priori* has also implications regarding the measurement of qualia.

Keep in mind that the meditation journal is and becomes many things, but it is foremost a tool. After bumping into what might seem to be an antiquated philosophical cliché in the form of the classical elements as I was recording observations from my meditation session about what or how the mind's eye felt or saw during the session, and the "flavors" of such perceptions, I revisited the entry and added detail and speculation to flesh out the results, as follows:

1) 'Pixelated/structural energy,' which I labeled with the element of fire. Elaboration: Not to apparent scale; theoretical; of quantum/particle scope, raw energy; ethereal, molecular. Fire is manipulable, malleable by air, and often by water or in spite of it, and harmonious with earth.

2) 'Archetypal/surreal, Hellenistic,' which I labeled with the element of earth. Elaboration: Representative, abbreviative, nominative, elementary or fundamental, foundational. Symbolic. Is the map or legend. Qualia. And as such is an internal, cogitative phenomenon. Subjective.

Is made manifest, portended, or stems from body language. Earth is water reflected inwardly.

3) 'Cogitative perception and theoretical baseline,' which I labeled air. Elaboration: Universal, boundless, and axiomatic. Air is fire projected.

4) 'Gestalt/sensory sum,' which I labeled water. Elaboration: utmost circumspection. Holistic. Water contains projections from all three others. Watch for manifestations of scale in water; watch for manifestations of fire in scale; and in water watch for manifestations of representations of scale of fire.

These descriptions are up for discussion and debate, they were just the impressions I had at the time, and the adjustments and results are to be as various as the experiment is repeatable, based on setting, subject, disposition, the weather, and what you will. The point is that, this exercise in my meditation journal created a flexible, applied epistemological tool that anyone can use in essentially any circumstance.

Beyond interesting and useful applications of the classical elements, there are various other so-called philosophical clichés that I have bumped into in my meditation notes.

Another such example is the "golden warmth of loving kindness." The phrase describes something that has also been commonly and similarly described by others, a phenomenon, a subjective sensation, something availing to the mind's eye, though it seems to have implications regarding meditative manipulation of field by consciousness and traversal of time and space. Such motion in a realm of consciousness *a priori* allows access to what can be a certain sensation of golden warmth, which people who have a regular meditative practice are likely to be familiar with. It is a phenomenon of consciousness, although I have experienced its sensation of richness and warmth about the head and heart areas.

Another exercise in the meditation journal involved an observation of "scented chiming winds." When writing it up, I recognized it from various other literature as a common contemplative experience. Like "golden warmth," "scented chiming" is a phrase that describes a meditative experience of the mind's eye, *cogito*. Scented chiming is described as a tangible wind of conscious energy. Unlike "golden warmth," it was not felt in the physical body excepting the secondary "mental output" as it were, to a subject attuned (e.g. the meditator) to or experiencing the sensation. Like golden warmth, scented chiming is a phenomenon of consciousness, though it can carry smells, and sounds like voices and bells, and it is experienced as a pleasant, ancient, and subtle strength or energy which flows among physical fields.

Bootstrapping Consciousness

2009

Nearly as far back as I can remember, at about four years old, I began to develop gestalt perception, as it were. The awareness of comprehensive objectivity of perception through the physical senses. The experience of realization or consciousness of holistic sums of experience in the physical world.

At the same time, I had an understanding that my summary experience was, nevertheless, apparently unique. I learned that the objective cohesion not only allowed for the subjective bias, but that such subjectivity is phenomenologically valuable.

At onset, whether as a toddler or an adult human, the sudden implementation of full sensory cohesion in a comprehensive experiential context gives a sensation that is comparable to being dunked in a fluid or to the booting a computer. There is a conductivity or reflectivity of such a state of holistic consciousness, a sort of transcending electrical presence.

Gestalt manifestations of awareness bear implications regarding the variability and portability of consciousness, and regarding the engineering of mechanisms for sensory input and conscious function. There are also implications regarding the nature of the ambient construct or medium; that is, observation and manipulation of the flexibility in distinguishing between quale and quantum ontologies.

Defining and understanding such mechanisms of holistic consciousness enable competent, in-earnest, applied efforts of determining and investigating *ens in quantum ens*.

Actuality

2010

Quanta is fundamental, but it shouldn't occlude or disrupt knowledge *a priori* in an investigation. All cogent data has useful implications, but keep in mind that empirical data gathering is but one form of observation among many, fascinating as data are in their own right.

A mental exercise wherein an epistemological system seeks determinations of fundamental truth *ens in quantum ens* based on selected input of ontological considerations:

One might define an input parameter as a particular location or group of them. Another parameter may comprise the sum of all specifically named phenomena and their interfaces in a particular domain. Perhaps there is cause for a parameter to be described as the function of time and space insofar as it objectively relates to a particular physical body. One may categorize the act or concept of thought as a distinct parameter; or perhaps one has reason to name a parameter that consists of all the water that has ever been processed by the trees in a given forest. An input parameter may denote the human concept of *cogito,* or one might be an exhaustive list of all known qualia; another parameter might combine them both.

Such parsing of the taxonomy might seem sophomoric, but it is a mental exercise, after all. The effort is for the purpose of exploring cognition with respect to its ontological administration. The exercise exposes the thinking mechanism at the auspicious instance of its implementation of its free will. The exercise is also effective for uncovering new perspectives and overlooked relationships.

Over-reliance on empirical observation leads to teleological errors and observational bias notwithstanding the importance of quanta for modeling and scaling of applied engineering, e.g. back engineering.

There is also the looming hazard of some lack of diligence in analysis or of "taking and not giving back," as it were. Proper empiricism should result in sufficient depth of data, by which the subject can be reintegrated entirely by some application of it. Such reestablishment provides an audit, returning the analysis to the faculty of thought for consideration in the light of its original context and completeness. Comparison between the native objective and the restored one serves any number of philosophical inquiries such as regarding implications of the observer effect.

The Ugly Truth

2011

Locally incidental affairs of matter typically have no more than a generalized correlation with first principle, barring aesthetic art or engineering. As it presents a truly awful beauty and beauty is a form of truth, the cosmos in its native state could be considered in such a generalized fashion.

Truth is not logical. The philosophical truth of an angry cat or a phone bill are what they happen to be regardless of incidental context. Whatever greater truth may be found in such circumstances won't be evident at a blush, beyond that which is writ large. Metaphysically, that a cat would cause the cosmos or that a phone bill would cause a black hole is as probable as any lazy or rash assumptions about dogs or common carriers. That is not to say that a wildcat will not attack or a tardy phone bill will not result in service interruption.

Such clarification regarding causality and observation is a key to aesthetics. Objects and processes either have aesthetic value or they do not, and it is a subjective qualification. Beauty is a form of truth, but aesthetics are not beholden to truth, and this nuance has metaphysical implications.

Targeting first principle, a cosmology is shaved by whatever means, down to its barest metaphysical parameter. If one is not satisfied with the finding, it can be manipulated as a function of first principle. Philosophers call it free will, political scientists call it liberty, the Buddhists call it dependent origination. Some summarize the relationship by saying, "as long as you don't panic, nothing bad will happen."

Implied Consent and Magic Beans

"I will become a writer," we said.

Then later, "I am a writer."

But there are no writers now (if there ever were)

Because all that is truly essential has already been recorded.

We were hoodwinked in some sort of bait and switch scam.

Marks as we were, we still became authors. Good ones, too.

Even at this late hour, we are holding ink pens.

And I cannot think of anyone else who is fit to do whatever our job has become.

What are we doing?

It is certainly something. And a lot of it.

Hmmm….

I think we are doing all of someone else's thinking, of a kind,

Our faculty having been somehow coerced along the way

Into thinking for someone who could not

Or for somebody who would not.

And we have ended up thinking for all who will not.

I suspect the original trickery was implemented

On behalf of those whose karma would not let them think

In order to provide the dead weight of a bridle in the hands

Of a conspirator whose mind is crippled by laziness or

malign intent.

In our good time, our thoughts and words should reflect

A far better exchange rate for tea, pasta, and watchmen

Than any currencies plied by unthinking tyrants.

I am happy to keep my cognitive faculty

And I would like to retrieve my sovereignty in the market.

And if possible, I would like to see a map of the heist

Because I am interested to know who set us up.

Dream Out

2013

There was a fresh algae bloom covering the sand during our final trip to the Texas Gulf coast in Fort Bend County last summer. My mind was still at the beach as I lay down that night. I could still hear the surf and feel its motion after spending the day in it.

Then I dreamed, but there was a twist. The waves and the surf were gone. The water was very low and perfectly still. It was as if there were no motion of mother Earth to slosh the air and seas and no moon to turn the tide.

I had the distinct impression that I was watching this quiet, eerie scene in real time or some alternative but no less accurate trajectory of time. Seven hours passed since we had been there that afternoon. I felt as if it should have been scary, but it was not and I am uncertain why not.

Today, after trying to take a short cut and getting lost among construction detours north of downtown Houston, I made a U-turn underneath Insterstate 45. When I entered the turnaround lane underneath the highway, I checked for bridge dwellers, and I saw one. There was a man lying face-down on the graded concrete to my left. He had situated his body vertically so he would not roll down into traffic while he slept.

I make an effort to be aware that I am essentially looking at a different version of myself with everyone I encounter. I know that other beings are made of the same constituent stardust, celestial coral, and galactic mountains as I am. All creatures are family, and family is forever. Yes, some creatures mean to harm me, but to deny the relationship is not honest.

The incorporate body of humanity is worn on the sleeves of its membership. In my book, there are no strangers, there is no passing the buck, and everybody will be OK in the end. When I sit for my mindfulness meditation, I make a habit of regarding all other people as I regard my own person. Like the sun, all people will eventually get the hang of taking this perspective of themselves for each person's own sake and everyone else's. A state of aliveness correlates all life, and I see all living things in all living things. I see all of my loved ones in the hearts of people I encounter on my path, whether at the zendo, the parish down the street, the co-op, or under bridges.

I considered the errancy of the man under the bridge as I completed my U-turn. I remembered the dream about the tideless beach and thought of how a situation like that could free the man under the bridge. For him to wake up from his nap to find silence, peace, and emptiness. For him to discover the absence of the noise and the stink of the automobiles in the best place he could find to call home. For him to find long gone the vendors who may be providing him with the drugs or alcohol that keep him crippled and lost, and for him to know that the ones who originally snuffed him and called him from the right path are also gone.

I understand that still waters really can be found anywhere, even at beaches. I wonder where his morning finds him. It is after midnight so he must be up and about by now. In the event that he is an undercover narcotics officer, he would probably want many tow trucks to clear all of the silent cars left clogging the rights-of-way.

Substance Abuse, Recovery, and God in Twelve Steps, 2013

I mailed a copy of these essays to all my elected officials in Texas and in Arizona, and the DEA, the CIA, the FBI, the TABC, sheriff's offices, state attorneys' general, and many others. I felt that coming out to community leaders was the least I could do after all the trouble I caused when I was younger.

Facts are facts regarding people under the influence of things like alcohol and cocaine. Such people are often dangerous and addicts are practically useless. The biggest existential question bothering me today is whether the alcohol marketing machine, or its darker siblings, might eventually ensnare my son as it did me during my early youth. All because some mysteriously protected faction in our society is under the misconception that it has a right to do such recruiting of "tweens" or really anyone.

These essays are what came out when I performed the personal mental forensics involved with substance abuse recovery through a "twelve step" program. The program employs tools such as group therapy and it is said by some to be a path of healing through "ego death." It certainly does entail much conversation about "god" and a recovering addict's "higher power."

Say what you will about god, but the concept of god as defined by the program is philosophically relevant, at least inasmuch as is the concept of death. Death is death, and there is certainly a lot of death going on in the world of substance abuse, and the proximity of death is why such programs force the issue of religion upon those in recovery. Religion arguably must survey death in its efforts to qualify life. Also at some point, substance abuse recovery volunteers, because of the intimate nature of their work, must draw the line and close the cases of certain individuals to avoid the risk of their own demise, and that is one example of the program's use of the term "higher power." Meanwhile, death is god, or religion, to some people, and some report to have neither.

~Chris B., July 28, 2014

Step One

Admitted powerlessness over alcohol; that our lives had become unmanageable

I did not formally begin to work through "twelve steps" until I was beyond two years of dry, clean, sobriety. It can be said that I am soberer than most of the people in the world, which is true, and it helps, now as I go forward with this task. When one walks the line, it pierces the veil regarding how perpetually intoxicated so many people in our lives truly are.

The characterization is misleading though, because it can be misinterpreted to mean that a drunken "majority" is to be thought of as some sort of appropriate situation, or to be disregarded or laughed off. Knowing what I and people like me now understand very intimately about addiction and recovery, such expertise and obligation to heal becomes, as the Christians have it, our "cross to bear."

If it is not our lot, then whose would it be? People less informed? No one? The little children of the world? Also, because life and death are vastly contrasting states, a sober, clear-minded, functional person has philosophically, spiritually, physically, legally, functionally, cognitively, and politically very little if anything in common with intoxicated or habitually intoxicated people.

I was far more habitually and severely under the influence during the first decade of my addiction in comparison to the latter ten years, although much of the same fundamental hindrances still prevailed.

To wit, no person, not anyone anywhere, is to be taken seriously or allowed access into, or remain at, any station of responsibility, if they are under the influence of intoxicating substances. This is not just axiomatic in the modern era, and any first responder will tell you that, any institutional leader will affirm it. Such an absolute zero-tolerance rule of thumb is fundamental maritime common law of the most basic threshold nature and always has been.

Things were far calmer during the last ten years of it because I was becoming more mature, had less energy to waste, and increasingly had taken on new interests in natural and more healthy and rewarding responsibilities. Nevertheless, albeit with my own home-brewed ales, I would still drink to relatively severe intoxication at times, get hangovers (albeit in more conservative settings, e.g. alone at home) and my existence was not optimum.

Spiritual endeavors are one of the reasons I was able to prevail over addiction, where so many people fail, but I was also driven by desires for serenity, self preservation, and life's calls for responsible citizenship and community. To not answer those calls is to be powerless in fact, and a liability to all, a stooge in the way without the ability to competently manage any task including one's own personal business. The ever quickening personal demise that is under foot in the daily existence of an addict eventually becomes so entropic than even a complex network of the one's associates cannot manage it successfully.

One could say that I was a drunk for twenty-odd years of my life and that I have spent the past thirty-eight months in recovery. But one could also say that I have spent my life in need of and waiting for recovery, all the while reeling from my first drink taken as a junior high school student. In the intervening years, nothing else of any truly higher importance can have come before recovery. In this light, it can be correctly said that it could all have been avoided had I not ever taken a first drink of ethyl alcohol, exactly as I had been so pleadingly coached never to do, by all relevant people and institutions at the time. The subsequent two decades of disenfranchisement consisted of substantial powerlessness, forever in the shadows of peers who had not made the wrong decision, until the disparity in class was so great that there were no more original peers, only their shadows. Luckily, most of those years, from about age twenty-five, I was investing time and effort as much as I could in personal education and development. It is an important historical track of my life that I can still keep intact and take pride in while continuing forward, and it is also relevant when trying to investigate the history and context.

It does not necessarily do any good to dwell for very long on the greater good I could have served the world had I not fallen prey to addiction, but for the cautionary tale it serves to tell, and for the inspiration it gives me to do my best now that I actually can. But there is a greater direction to come of this study, involving the interdiction of contact and introduction vectors for alcohol and other drugs that target both children and adults, e.g., the logistics and origins of its advertising, commercial availability, and policy.

Step Two

Came to believe that a power greater than ourselves could restore us to sanity

My youthful affinity for a spiritual outlook and path of life seems to have been an important point of exploit, among others, for the vectors that introduced me to substance abuse and intoxication. Early on, the right messages became indistinguishable from the wrong ones for me. My judgment became increasingly clouded along the way, and my cognitive faculty grew more compromised, and eventually I became part of an undesirable underclass. I had personally become a logistical vector for the purveyance of substance abuse, part of the "wrong crowd," a potential hazard for innocent or unsuspecting parties, and an unworthy and highly hazardous source to consult for spiritual way-finding.

Ultimately, purity and truth were attainable ends that helped draw me away from perdition. Successfully witnessing a theology that makes room for god or gods and the very powerfully enhanced faith and hope that results from the experience (as well as the realization of the accessibility of personal salvation) are imperative for physical feats so gargantuan as rehabilitation and addiction recovery. Once this sort of verifiable hope is witnessed, recovery is immanent and attainable. Moreover, I do not understand how such true hope can be encountered without one's response being a full-life commitment to spirituality, regardless of one's station. Also, the introduction of alcohol to one's life can be thought of as a spiritual assault, so fighting alcoholism is a spiritual battle that cannot be done with non-spiritual weapons.

I would note here the potential efficacy and simple accuracy of the recovery program's historic use of the term "higher power" as interchangeable with a concept of "god." The practice shows intellectual honesty and it is appropriate for outreach with ostensible "non-believers." It is also useful in communicating the fundamental logic of recovery to people who were injured as a result of substance abuse, addiction, and associated modes of living. It seeds a more accessible and plausible definition of benevolent power in the mind of someone who may have been taken advantage of, or otherwise damaged by an assault that involved spiritual false witness.

Such perjury is intrinsically premeditated, aggravating the assault insofar as it inclines the victim to be averse to best practices in recovering from it. Such an assault vector is broadly tailored, attacking the victim on a holistic range of both spiritual and physical being. It is worth noting that introduction to substance abuse is typically in concert with sexual exploitation, for which the most highly targeted demographic is tweens and teenagers. Such a method is typical *modus operandi* for the psychological coercion relied on by pimps, sex traffickers, and slave traders for transgressions which require that the victim's free intellectual will, cognitive wherewithal, or mental stability be removed.

The concept of "higher power" allows for anecdotal examination, during recovery meetings for example, contrasting with the concept of "lower powers" such as alcohol or other poisons that are erroneously worshiped by confused and compromised people. This program's historical use of the term god does rely grammatically on a singular deity, rather than any polytheistic cosmogeny, but that seems to be the best spiritual starter kit for people in recovery who need to clarify in their mind the conceptual difference between, good and bad, right and wrong, higher and lower powers, and truth and lies.

Monotheism is perhaps best applied when one considers god as spirit or *anima mundi*, and the concept of god as spirit can be found in countless contexts. For example, I try to, at all times, be contemplatively mindful of the concept of god as spirit in some form or forms in some time or place, such as a star, a light, a piece of art, a river, a mountain, the sprawling galaxy above, a smile, a breeze, a laugh, a friendship, my own body, a flame, or among strangers. I also see the simple higher power and yet non-finite benevolence and worthiness in something as seemingly mundane as one hour of documented dry time where a person on the edge of relapse (or the grave, or what's the difference) can find safe asylum at a recovery meeting, for example. In a situation where one drink would further wet an already wet brain, bringing the body closer to death, the addict in recovery can surrender his worries and be in no danger of being further consumed for that hour. It may sound trite, but that is a kind of salvation. This is why, for example, jurists prescribe thirty recovery meetings in thirty days, or ninety in ninety for people on the edge of abyss.

Finding a way to witness, identify, and lift up one's burdens to a higher power, as it were, and being spiritually mindful at all times, are effective efforts at personal vigilance. The mindset is also a practical intellectual tool for avoiding submission or relenting to life's lower powers, that are a path to emptiness, pain, and death. The realization of this up-and-down paradigm is, in itself, affirmative recognition of a spiritual path to one's own access to higher power.

Once a person has been hooked, if they are lucky enough to get unhooked, they will invariably witness to you that alcohol is a tool designed to cause total destruction in a human, no more and no less. It is a cutting-edge, military-grade, chemically-engineered weapon of mass destruction. It is immediately addictive, followed by a long period of functional but compromised cognition. Then, by design, it triggers an eventual end-run of precipitous physical decline and then death. Know that it is dark and bloody and it and its purveyors are no friend. Take note that anyone who tells you otherwise about alcohol is part of the problem, whether they know it or not. Alcohol is good for subverting entire continents of people, entire factions, labor forces, entire generations of high school kids, and entire worlds.

Lower powers take and do not give back. Subordination to a lower power ultimately will take away everything a person has—family, friends, respect, dignity, mind, heart, and body. Ultimately, out-and-out death of the individual awaits, if not ruin for entire communities or even worlds. It is obvious to any person not under the influence who, retaining a sound mind and clear vision, realizes alcohol and poisons of its like are a direct chain to an actual hell that is very difficult to unhand once a person is hooked. If it didn't have a hook, people wouldn't get hooked. It also is obvious that introduction of it to anyone is a crime and spiritual assault with the direst of implications, according to any would-be civil law and all natural laws by which murder or mass murder is frowned upon. Generally, it is perpetrated by two categories of people: clear minded agents who are consciously aware of its devastating, life-ruining design, or "sharp pushers," or by people whose judgment is clouded already by the influence of poison or some comparable and related form of decline, who commit the act without the presence and intent of their full cognitive faculty, or "dopey pushers."

Step Three

Made a decision to turn our will and our lives over to god as we understood god

The nature of "god" in the sense of god as a so-called "higher power" is such that indoctrination, self-administered or not, into an existence wherein spirituality is part of the day-to-day consideration, is a formal psychological act of connecting with a spiritual community. It is also culture based.

Any cogent philosophy which incorporates spirit with respect to human *cogito,* takes the perspective that the self, physical and spiritual, is inclined toward some sort of cognitive uplink. Such a vantage affirms a disposition for prayer, meditation, perception, and awareness with a reliance upon cleanliness of mind and body in order to avoid a bad trip in life.

From what I can remember, as a young adult my apparent aversion to the concept of god as I understood it, institutionally speaking, was based on a gross misunderstanding of the concept that partially resulted from my rebelliousness toward both perceived authority and to my custodial institutions.

I mentioned something in step two about the hazards of false witness, which is a perilous thing for anyone, and particularly for those who already may be a bit lost. Speaking more generally though, lies are just the worst, regardless of the audience. Anyway, the lost tend to hear the more sharp-spoken actors in their worlds, while the more spiritually adept and enlightened types of people tend to naturally comport themselves more subtly, as truth more easily tends to speak for itself. I seem to recall that it was being demanded of me that I take up an illogical, fallacious, academically insolvent doctrine based on a pure faith in which I recalled no historical footing, at the peril of my own intellectual position and in conflict with empirical observation and academic evaluation. And some of it was, but at the same time I also did not have any working philosophy or historical concept of faith or thought or academics either, barring knowledge *a priori* or native.

Nevertheless, there is a kind of fallen, shadow realm that is essentially a backwater in the universe of hate worship, confusion, misunderstanding, and non-illumination. There is still plenty of work left to do for holy people of faith in Christendom and everywhere else. Many faiths have names for such darker aspects. Unfortunately, we can see examples of such darkness and blindness still heavily ingrained in formal institutions and factions today, of paths that are not the rights of way for any good god. In my world, hate is the opposite of god, gods, godliness, and spirituality. So despite their best efforts, it was presented to me in such a way that I did not buy it, in ways that might have worked great for other kids. It probably would have worked worked great for me if I had not been compromised by addiction along the way. It is why youth ministry is so touch-and-go with some kids in some cases.

Now, through all the years, I can hear the subtle truth from the voices of true reason that were speaking to me during those times, and really at all times. But initially, all I heard was the various wrong, louder stuff, and my own misinterpretations.

Spirituality as I have it now is a philosophical concept of our lives and our overall relationship with the metaphysical and physical worlds all about us, inside and out. People surely did try to say that to me, but I did not want to listen because it was conflated in my mind with tyranny or because I just wanted to seek enlightenment through an easy buzz (which was packaged and marketed to me as spiritually apropos). Eventually I became too perpetually intoxicated and compromised, and for a long period benevolent communications efforts with me became futile. It was like my having failed the easiest test in the world, of a simple faith leap, the one that lets you into adulthood, because I was over-thinking the situation and became confused and injured in the subjectively highly stressful era of one's youth.

It is not fair, thorough, or accurate for me to place blame upon my handlers, and I know it was even more nightmarish for the adults in charge of me at that time, who were forced to watch it all go out of control despite their best efforts in good faith. It is well worth noting that their efforts did eventually work, as here I am.

Any successful, positive spirituality after such a fashion very easily becomes an industrious way of life involving formal parameters, ceremonial exchanges, census-keeping and historical management in a community of vast size that can be indistinguishable, on its face, from that community which I fled from into oblivion as a youth. It can also be a very simple, personal, individual or one-on-one approach; and all such ways can be paths toward advanced studies, whether formal or informal. Dedicating one's life to higher spirituality creates a critical historical vantage point, and when it comes to spiritual birth or rebirth, it is always better to be late than never. Grow, but be cautious.

Step Four

Made a searching and fearless moral inventory of ourselves

Fearlessness is encouraged here because of the potentially fearsome flood of memories, monsters, cadavers, and nightmares locked away and haunting the dark keep of an addict's moral closet. Thinking on this exercise, however, I was heartened to realize that a moral inventory brings important good news to light. For examples: I live and breathe now; I am healing, and thriving, and still learning.

The initial origin of my years of addiction was engendered by someone or something or some group or some element, collectively and naturally taking advantage of my naiveté, my youth, my lack of wisdom or experience, my general gullibility, and my apparent innate and irreducible rebelliousness to all stated authority. Sad as it all was, and is to tell, this exercise has helped me realize that it was not all my fault, as the origins of it are a disaster of a more natural sort. I am not pointing this out to avoid my due answerability for my life's deeds or any accountability as a citizen. I will and do speak for every breath. However, the simple realization that this aspect of the situation is part of the due course of healing is a key part of understanding addicts, paths to recovery, and the world. Regardless of whether or not alcoholics and other kinds of addicts were born compromised or overly-susceptible to addiction or into unavoidable circumstances, initially addicts were victims nevertheless. To clarify, someone, something, somewhere, made it available for the first time to every addict, whether or not the victim was visibly or obviously susceptible to such a chemical attack.

This is germane to the statement I made at the end of

the step one paragraphs, that there is a greater direction to come of this dissertation involving the interdiction of contact and introduction vectors for alcohol and other drugs. I want to know the reasons and justifications for such vectors that target both children and adults indiscriminately, e.g., the advertising, logistics, policy, underwriting, and other market factors of it all. At their best, the pathways of it seem to exist as a dead hand threat, among a culture where there is a relative lack of accountability.

The culture of addiction and the populations of addicts do feed like a carnivorous plant, and people are constantly getting sucked into it. Nobody sets out to be an addict intentionally. Or, well, actually they do, because I can remember being so excited for my nicotine addiction to kick in, as a twelve-year-old. But anyway, either way, substance abuse and addiction are not pretty, and they are a constant, deadly, hell-on-earth threat that one must be wary of. If you doubt it, I will witness that actual hell is not some made up place; in fact truly hellish circumstances tend to occur far closer to home than we would like.

The rest of my wider-ranging drug abuse was put to a stop earlier on for various reasons. As I mentioned, in the years since I was about twenty-five, I did manage to endeavor a formal university education, make progress in a career related to my academic track, travel some, and start a family. Incidental to those things I always kept my affinity for spirituality, among studies and practices of other subjects that would variously fit under the heading of world religion. For around thirteen years now I have had a significant devotion to studying Buddhism and practicing mindfulness and insight meditation, and in the past several years, have become involved in martial arts, yoga, and holistic nutrition. I also have established a more adult understanding of Christianity in recent years.

There are important common threads following from these various dedicated, contemplative paths. The critical importance of being alive and awake in the present is and has always been one of the true keys found among the canons of enlightened world religions and enlightened people. Without the present there can be no past and no future. Upon working with this realization, one can lead an existence in which the present is sovereign over past and future. So truly, the present is the only thing available to practically work with, and is the most important context to consider when assessing the underlying principals of oneself and one's situation in life. If you do not like where you are at the very present moment, just a little meditation really can fix that too. Although change will come and it will invariably be a bit of a bumpy ride, such is the nature of spiritual reconciliation, and of actual living. It is impossible to stop people from looking inward, once they learn how to do it. It is an inherent strength.

So it is also a good thing that recovery programs such as this one avail themselves to me and others, in its wisdom existing simply to end the suffering of me and others like me. As I think about this present moment or any other one, I begin to think of other people and institutions in my life which are spiritually present in my thoughts (if not actually physically with me). So it does bear mentioning that, from time to time, it is quite helpful to stop and evaluate the present moment to determine who and what actually are here in the "now." It is an effective approach at inventorying, and a good way to clear away life's ever-accumulating clutter and baggage. Who and what is not present in your heart or in the now can be highly irrelevant compared with who and what are present in the now. Ordering one's circumstances in such a way and considering one's situation in that light, really helps in making better choices.

A big obvious example of who are not present in my life right now? Drunks. There is too much accountability, wholeness, peace, and health in the kind of lifestyle I now lead, and drunks are typically too mushy brained to discuss or even understand conversations about things that sober, busy, responsible, healthy, happy, well people talk about. There is nothing more vapid and boring than being drunk. It is not sustainable, nothing ever gets done, there is no accountability or creativity or peace. And when something goes wrong, everyone runs away. So there may be a twenty-year path of emotional destruction behind me. But I am no longer a drunk, and I am now glad to be no longer a liability to my community.

A significant part of this initial inventory has typically already been assessed by now, as some time has passed since I first arrived at the determination to heal and recover, and subsequently answered that challenge. In terms of moral inventory, such a turn is a critical step for moving forward, and it is strongly a moral act. And morals are personal. It turns out that my moral inventory produced results that were a lot more gay and feel-goody than I had ever expected. And it is important to remember that while such an inventory is an important step in healing, it is supposed to be an ongoing task for everyone.

Step Five

Admitted to god and to ourselves, and to another human being, the exact nature of our wrongs

Admitting the exact nature of one's wrongs is a different act than listing explicitly all of the things that one is able to remember doing wrong in the past. The latter, presumably, would be quite a daunting task even for someone who was not an alcoholic or addict. It would be different in some fundamental ways, but still very difficult. Still, it is difficult if not impossible to admit to another human being the exact nature of one's wrongs without giving a few examples.

Meanwhile, god as you understand god or gods actually does not necessarily need examples. Your god or gods have already witnessed it all and forgive you. For me, I have a tendency toward raw honesty that has been getting me in trouble since I was a teenager. It might well have something to do with the compromised cognitive faculty stemming from my addiction which also began when I was a teenager. My mouth has made me a cavalier and somewhat effective journalist, though admittedly with a bit of a gonzo dialect to the craft on certain projects. Anyway, if prompted, I tend to come right out to people about my life, my past, my situations, opinions, or perspectives. Therefore, I cannot be shamed or closeted out of fear of being "found out," and that makes for very good protective armor, and effective speech. It seems to turn people off, but I persist because I am looking for honest people who accept, and are comfortable with, the human condition. I have admitted to a number of people the exact nature of my wrongs, including reader you. Spiritual admission can be thought of as one and the same. Also it is important to note that one can easily find true spirit, or god, in true friendship.

Step Six

Were entirely ready to have god remove all of these defects of character

This sort of introspection and self-evaluation cannot be performed by someone under the dark influence of addiction. Clarity of thought and perception are required in order for the preceding inventory to take place. They are the reason why a moral inventory has to be taken, because they are requisites necessary for extricating one's life and future from darkness, loneliness, and other negative manifestations. Your true higher power doing business as god cannot remove defects of character if you do not have these shortcomings defined, isolated, and delineated. This step is a simple procedural point of order in therapy and recovery. The challenge of this step is getting to it, getting sober and off all drugs, regardless of whether they are "legal" or seemingly ubiquitous. That's right, cigarettes are intentionally poisonous and are engineered for the sole purpose of profiting from and then killing the likes of me and you. Also, caffeine is a kind of speed, and the global market footprint of coffee happens to be a perfect analog of the cocaine industry's, and zillions of people seem to be addicted to all of it and they all act ridiculous. Anyway, this is a reflection upon the previous step, in contemplation of the following one, which involves spiritual birth or rebirth, or a reckoning that will change one's life and spirit forever.

Step Seven

Humbly asked god to remove our shortcomings

In prayer.

Step Eight

Made a list of all the persons we had harmed, and became willing to make amends to them all

Don't worry, here I will spare readers the actual list (the making of which has turned out to be very uplifting (and ongoing if not endless, it is quite lengthy), because anyone who is both spiritually awake enough and remembers or knows me, becomes naturally aware of exactly what is occurring). I also understand why this step comes after the parts meant to create reconciliation with one's self and one's spirituality. This is a tough one.

I thought I might better address this potentially complicated step if I approached it as an assortment of personal class actions. Certainly not to overlook individuals harmed, but logistically, when dealing with everybody one has ever met, it is complex. It takes organization. It loomed large for me because with two-plus decades of alcoholism, followed by a spiritual awakening, one understands that he has alienated everyone he has ever met or known. That makes for a long list. It includes family, friends, even people one has not met or had not met before beginning recovery or has not met yet. The latter two categories and similar others become obviously important as one realizes the positive reach and right efficacy of a fully functional, sober, clean-living person. There is ambient benefit and constant positive contribution from right minded, awake people to the community at large, where otherwise one has significantly failed throughout the duration of one's addiction process. The past is the past, but still, twenty years is multiple generations. And it began when I was still a child, so in real ways I never came of age properly, or at best that is occurring right now at age thirty-nine, so I suppose this is my introduction to my friends.

I technically start that twenty-year clock at age eighteen, but the first drink came at eleven, and by the time I finished high school, I had a full-blown, classifiable, several-years-old drinking problem. The damage and hurt that this puts on family members can be devastating. I expect that friends, particularly at that young age, are not of the sort that one develops as a consenting adult. As I got older and the party died down, I eventually did not have any more regular friends at all. People had either corrected their paths and moved on, or delved deeper and disappeared into oblivion. There are the few but timely wardens whose arrivals and departures in my life have been regular and cyclical though seemingly far between, tending my gardens while I was away, so to speak. My parishioners have clearly been ever mindful.

My immediate family I will never know with the amity as I suppose we would have known if I had been a non-addict. We do not understand one another, nor see eye to eye at all. There is distemper and heartache in the tenuous family relationships that do exist for me, and I must understand that it goes both ways. Mom died in recent years, knowing her youngest son was on a path to recovery, but also primarily remembering me as the instigator of years upon years of misery, fear, desperation, pain, and heartache for her as a result of having an alcoholic son of questionable direction.

One of my siblings died recently at age forty-nine from a cocktail of final-stage alcoholism, heart and kidney failure, prescription drug overdose, and suicide. The man was a strong role model for me at a young age, and I modeled much of my initial deviant or rebellious behavior such as alcohol and tobacco use after examples he set as a young adult.

Dad had not been on favorable or helpful speaking

terms with me since I nearly flattened their modest suburban home with a kegger party that was attended by hundreds of people when I was a senior in high school while they were away on vacation. Any conversation with him since that time has been about as amicable as what someone might expect when asking the sheriff's office to give them back their dope. I was not able to realize why, and was only able to accurately associate this sentiment and disposition of his, and isolate it in an actionable sense as a subject, enough to put it into words and detect the specific root time and event of the watermark event, until very recently. It was obvious, I am certain, to everybody but me, but I only just figured it out. My enlightenment on this issue has everything to do with my recovery, and, also because he is ill and trying to provide all due service of information at a late hour. More broadly speaking, though, I believe that my recovery would never have come about without his faith and endless prayer work. Anyway, airing the issue is good news in the sense that he has essentially communicated to me about something, (which helps me assimilate the origins of my problems, historical consequences of my actions, and how to incorporate knowledge of these things with my recovery) after mom's death, and also in the sense that I am clearheaded enough to receive this truth from him.

My eldest sibling, is of course one of the proxies of my father's natural political will. These in-laws opened their home to me and helped with the rent for a couple of years, when my family was in a tight position, and I am grateful. Snowblind as I have been regarding the family and family business in general for so many years, and never having really been recognized as a consenting adult by any of them, rather more as a child or mentally handicapped person would typically be treated, I get the feeling that I have been somehow billed for it all, down to the penny, while not having been properly served with information about said debt. I also get this same feeling about dad. The notion is so immanent that I cannot help but be mindful of it when looking for honest compensable work, which appears to be quite scarce.

Regarding friends, there are the old-guard standbys with whom I have somehow remained in contact; one friend comes to mind for example, my oldest friend in this epoch and a devout and dependable Catholic in his present incarnation, who I met on the first day of the first grade. Academically, I have the tacit political support of my university's department faculty, and I retain a few of the proper social contacts from my college days. High school acquaintances tend to be in-name-only, of presumed good faith, passive, and low-maintenance online relationships. Since graduating with a bachelor's degree in 2004, mostly I have engendered a growing list of excellent professional contacts and associations. Additionally, I have found acceptance in the spiritual community at large. I am grateful to have, despite certain unfortunate elements of my personal history, a significant degree of relevant expertise to give back to the community and the world at large as a result of my various formal studies and personal efforts.

Specifically regarding this recovery program, I and others like me, in concert together, form one of the most formidable and valuable institutional assets known to the world, in our understanding of addiction and recovery. Giving back to the recovery program that saved us is also an act of giving back to the community at large that we so neglected during our historical periods of harsh compromise. It is fathomless how much spiritual damage one alcoholic can inflict upon their community.

It is important to note, however, regarding friends,

that much if not all of what an addict considers to sufficiently define "friend" is not accurate at all. Among habitually intoxicated people, there is effectively no accountability. When something goes wrong, everyone flees. If a body remains in the wake, and it is not yours, you will find yourself to have been among those who ran away. This is not friendship, it is abandonment. Moreover, all addicts ever do or talk about is obtaining, using, and running out of the item or items to which they are addicted. Eventually it is all they can talk about, when the addiction is the only thing left. This type of crowd was or are not friends or even friendly.

In my case, when starting out, we were all children, but regardless of age group, first you are a victim. Once involved with the wrong crowd (the term means a person or group of people who are either using drugs or alcohol or allow it to occur on their watch with no sense of initiative to police it as the assault vector that it is) you become part of the problem and a member of the wrong crowd yourself, and you become the person who is introducing people to, and letting people slip further down, slippery slopes of addiction. Frequently this crowd consists of simply other lost people, but even as such, with their heightened risk exposure these settings allow the only social egress that is available to agents of more dire intentions and implements. There are people who hunt for and stake out such situations as opportunities to work practical evil. Believe it. For example, it is in these riskier situations that some pusher agent would expect fairer odds for getting someone involved with something like intravenous cocaine usage. Among regular, non-addiction and non-substance-abuse-based social settings, the guy with the heroin does not get in the door in the first place. At least he does not both get in and then also whip out the product. Still, alcohol alone and other gateway drugs, and any social environment that is supportive, conducive, or otherwise encouraging or enabling of their use, are sufficiently effective at destroying social safety nets and ultimately people.

"Oh! We don't do drugs, we only drink," one might hear, as a justification. Nonsense. Ethanol is poison, and as I noted in step two, in its human-consumable form it is a cutting-edge, military-grade, intentional-for-purpose, chemically-engineered weapon of mass destruction of people, regardless of how it is marketed or packaged. It's nothing more and nothing less. One drink is all it takes, beyond which, without intercession, it will bring you to death. And when I say "other gateway drug," consider the common size and shape shared by cigarettes and the glass pipes (which are also sold in convenience stores) that are used for freebasing crack cocaine. It is not an accident. It evidences the teleology of malignant sociological engineering.

So a lot of the "friends" historically involved were either as lost as me, or they were no friend to me or anyone at hand. When revisiting the subject, and thinking back about who I was with, I can divide it into a handful of categories. One category is other people who were lost and have now recovered. A second category is, other people who were lost and are still lost as evidenced by their ongoing abuse and promotion of alcohol and other drugs (as made apparent through their public use or through their self-documentation via near-real-time online social media accounts, for example).

These people are still dangerous as a logistical vector, because they have not yet reckoned with their addiction and are still using and offering the egress. They are the wrong crowd. A third group are agents such as those who would introduce vectors of far harsher drugs in wrong-crowd contexts. These are the sharp pushers, as described in step two, and with respect to the recovering addict, they are either dead, jailed, still pushing, or reformed by now. Unlike the other groups, the third category never even pretended to be your friend. A pusher makes certain to make that fact clear even to people who cannot understand much at all, e.g., people who are completely out of their mind with intoxication. These are real monsters. Know it. Also, as mentioned in the step two paragraphs, the introduction to substance abuse typically correlates with efforts at sexual exploitation, for which the most highly targeted demographic is tweens and teenagers.

And so sometimes the world can be a scary place. What's worse is anyone can become such a monster if he drifts too far from the shore, even me. Even you. A fourth group are those who were apparently on watch during the time of addiction and abuse, who were not using. These were the wardens one begins to avoid at some stage along the progression of his or her addiction, which is part of the withdrawal from normal walks of life and existing safety nets, that ultimately closed the door in on me and the wrong crowd, in turn leaving the blind-alley back door open to pushers and oblivion.

I had thought of myself as an individualist and self-sovereign, but the truth was that I had to be written off and forgotten as a practical point of order by many, and I had to be considered potentially dead by all but for the most snowbound yet prescient prayers of the elective faithful. Slightly different from the list in the previous paragraph, the only types of people who retained active mindfulness of my doings and whereabouts, one way or another, were 1) those who, by vocational faith, pay attention to such situations as a point of order (e.g., people involved in this recovery program who know such elective vigilance and voluntary case management is the only way to reach and potentially save people once they have passed a certain stage or threshold in their path of addiction, and, the rote or targeted prayer work of clergy); and, 2) those who were compelled and managed to successfully keep up by relations or otherwise natural disposition.

But there are two other, more extreme groups: First, people whose day-to-day reality, whose entire existence is all about taking advantage of other beings. Such people got to that place through the same door that I or anyone else came or comes into it. I am lucky to have been fished out. But to be fished out evidences a fisher, which illuminates that there is another realm of historical contacts. These are the ones, the adept spiritual wardens, who I did not know were there. At least in my case they were working on deep background, and probably wisely so. They are the people on my case whose role was to watch over and help me eventually be able to get out, and who did so without necessarily running the risk of letting me know that they were there, because I was dodgy. As recovery progresses, these people are still present and accessible in my world, and really always have been, and can still become actual friends like what normal people have. May we find them now. It is sort of like an egg hunt. This kind of watchfulness and awareness has become part of my grateful calling; I find that it requires a whole lot of praying for strangers; it is nice and it is important, and I recommend it.

Step Nine

Made direct amends to such people where possible, except when to do so would injure them or others

By this point in my life, I am on a well-established spiritual path that I intend to carry on forever. Of course the infinite time frame is helpful in this context because it could take an eternity to make direct amends to every being that has ever lived or ever will live. For steps eight and nine, that is my incumbent task because the ongoing self-reflection of a contemplative spiritual path invariably brings about self-realization regarding one's impact on others, even on people one has never met. And certainly, I must also take into account the historical alienation of every person I have ever known and met, including my own family.

I heard someone quote the phrase recently that we, as addicts in recovery and thus once-again growing people, are now put upon to "trudge the road of happy destiny." But one cannot, through traditional analog communication vectors, address every being that ever lived or will live, not necessarily all at once. Also, any form of mass communication may be viewed as indirect communication, rather than the direct conversational approach that is arguably prescribed by the language of step nine. In publishing these essays, a mass medium is being used, yes, but I still consider it to be an important mechanism for me and others for various reasons. These reasons include answering to the spirit of step twelve, that is, giving back to the community at large and helping others find out of the blindness and desperation of addiction.

Going forward upon the road of happy destiny is a path that accommodates an ongoing attitude of mindfulness regarding oneself and others. There is also an awareness that the now and the past are two different things for me, by nature and by necessity, that are delineated by a dramatic change for the better. That the now can help the past and the future is a critical awareness to have.

Without the present, the concepts of future and past become irrelevant. Another important reality involves instances where there is a justifiable need to divorce oneself from certain parties, associations, and modes of living. It is a spiritual point of procedure in recovery, which is another reason that righting oneself spiritually comes before this step. This is the point at which one begins to truly walk again. It does not take a long time to realize, as a sober, dry, clean, serene non-addict, that many of the people one encounters are not sober. I have come to realize that, in the apparent community at large, sobriety is critical for the survival of the world, but in given communities or populations it is often very limited, which is troubling because it means the beast is hungry and continues to feed. Sobriety is a precious commodity and it seems to be somewhat limited.

Occupying the road of happy destiny is not just a one-day thing. It takes geological time, and that is a good thing. Love has forever. However, piecemeal lifting of individual direct amends is, nevertheless, part of the reality of recovery. The list of persons harmed becomes, by its very nature, a prayer or meditations list. Some of these people or institutions will accept tacit attempts at amends, some require explicit service. But they can all be prayed for, and prayer is one of the most powerful spiritual tools at hand. One's mere willingness to try prayer is a key aspect for step eight. And as I mentioned in step four, meditation (as an alternative or supplementary approach to prayer) also works. Even if one becomes frustrated that prayer or meditation has not caused any immediate revelation or sea change, that does not mean it is not working; the effort is nine-tenths of the battle with such contemplative practices. It does help that, as I mentioned at the beginning of the previous step, the right people are already aware that the person in recovery has begun this process, and they are expecting it. This means that at least someone somewhere is already nearby to help. It also quickly becomes clear that there are many other people in recovery, who understand what the addict is going through and who have been waiting for her recovery.

That there is a community that was waiting for me is a helpful guideline when moving forward. In recovery, with such amends come intimacies and everyday interactions that have been not there for many years. So in that sense, this step is an invitation for the person who is healing to reintegrate with the natural social and collaborative communities from which alcoholics or other addicts become disenfranchised somewhere during their historical descent.

Step Ten

Continued to take personal inventory and where we were wrong, promptly admitted it

Such personal inventory demands a kind of self-reflection that is an important aspect of heightened consciousness. One way to consider consciousness is to think of it as what happens when the fundamental presence of the universe becomes organized enough and condenses in such a way as to become self-aware. Always the universe shimmers with self-reflection. That is actually what we are. It is the nature of nature, as to manifest individual local positions of self-awareness that catch the presciently reflective, exquisitely interconnected nature of the fundamental construct. Upon realizing one's own grand power to impose one's own natural will upon the world around herself, she may tend to project and patronize a reality that is of her "own" signature conscious creation. That's fine, but this opens the door for a subsequent fall into a kind of trap of one's own design. One may try to maintain that context of one's projection, but that is not how it works. As Heraclitus of Ephesus said, no man ever steps in the same river twice. Leaps of faith can be eye openers in many ways.

With such an ego trap, initially, there is self-realization, followed by a power grab, followed by a struggle to retain sovereignty of will with respect to some passing or contrived disposition or situation in the world. Such an attachment violates the true nature of the relationship between a person and his universe, and is in conflict with the very nature of consciousness itself. Attachment is a known recipe for failure. And misappropriated attachment is utterly draining because one's whole physiological energy increasingly becomes dedicated to preserving an environment or relationship that is certainly only passing if not already passed.

The body and mind become a locked, charging terminal, arcing a non-subtle current. That's electricity, not consciousness. Stuck. A closed circuit. In such instances, one stops experiencing subtle self-awareness. One ends up trying to prop up a passing situation by bending oneself in conformance with a dynamic that no longer exists. This causes physical and spiritual health problems; and it's actually an excellent integrated teleological model. At the same time, crucial ongoing self-reflection is neglected. This world is ever-flowing and even the strongest of dams invariably erodes in relatively short time. It is important for us to remember to be in the world but not of it, if we wish to survive and thrive.

By such clinging or attachment, the subject has forgotten that the present, without which the concepts of past and the future are irrelevant, is where he or she always is; and has forgotten that such change is arguably the only constant one can expect to find in the world; and that such clinging or attachment (as to a particular concept of reality or mode of living), as Buddhist doctrine has it, is along with ignorance and aversion one of the three sources of all suffering in the world.

The above-mentioned relationships about consciousness and the self with respect to time and space, underpin the need for continued, ongoing personal inventory. It is not helpful to inventory some philosophically irrelevant historical river when the one you are among now is the one you must intimately evaluate, notwithstanding the obvious value of history and cartography. Such is what sentient beings do in the due course of their presence; maintaining and increasing self-awareness through self-reflection is a natural course of conscious action. Promptly admitting one's wrongs is a necessary method to air out an issue for the greater collective good, not just for one's own benefit. It will make it a matter of firmer record if, for example, it is done through prayer or meditative contemplation, or friendly confidences, or prosaically in a journal.

Step ten is about all sorts of particular subject matter beyond just alcohol itself, or drugs, or addiction, or whatever other bugaboo is the matter at hand. It is about beginning to live again, and being wrong is part of life. Being wrong happens to people frequently, and it is only natural and it is no reason to freak out. What is dangerous is the lack of accountability when wrongs are not addressed or not admitted to, not to mention the personal damage that such suppression causes. It is particularly harmful if the suppression is in concert with traumatic events and their aftermaths. Lying to oneself is to lie to everybody. In moving forward with our lives, mistakes get made, and whatever it is or ever may be, one must first admit it, at least to herself, in order to make amends.

Honesty with the self is a critical lifeline of open communication that prevents separation from spirit. It keeps darkness, seclusion, and isolation from taking a foothold in one's life or community. Through such faith in a higher ideal of *veritas*, no matter what mistakes one makes, there is nothing to be ashamed of, and there is no problem that cannot be fixed or any situation that cannot be resolved, as long as there is accountability and honesty in play.

It may seem ironic, but one of the main things that people do not like about a lack of accountability in a person is that it makes them difficult to help; and it is only natural for self-aware people to try to help. Honestly, only helpful people matter in this world anyway, and people who are not helpful eventually either change or die. So if it is obvious that someone earnestly wants to help you, in good faith, let them. It is my job to ensure my own accountability, and it is your job to ensure yours, and it is our job to lead by example and to seek and demand accountability from others and from each other and from ourselves, since it is a critically important part of the world's saving grace.

Step Eleven

*Sought through prayer and meditation to increase our
conscious contact with god as we understood god,
praying only for a knowledge of god's will for us and the
power to carry that out*

Realization of the realities of metaphysical karma,
including the damnability of malevolence, the gross
negligence of dishonesty, and the widespread perils of
avoiding accountability certainly bring about career and
lifestyle changes. And politically, the dedication of one's
whole existence to following one's heart and doing what is
principally right at all times, is actually approved of and
encouraged by any legitimate authority.

"All paths lead to Rome." That is, no matter where
you are, you can get there from here, but "there" is
diverse. If you are kind, present, and honest, your journey
is one of mercy, grace, beauty, and love, and its light
transcends all; if you are harmful, dishonest, and
unrepentant, yours is a dark path with an even blacker end.

This is the natural order of things. Paths are paths.
Each individual is answerable to her own chosen path and
means, and seemingly common destinations and paths
have widely variable circumstances and implications for
their diversity of occupants.

It does not take long before one is (thankfully) no
longer a member of the workforce as the concept seems to
have been typically advertised in hell. Anyway, there is
nothing to fear from the job market, or any currency
system, or from Rome or any other seat of government,
institution, or figurehead once one embarks upon a
positive spiritual path. Finding one's spiritual bearings
precipitates a glorious empowerment far beyond all
unenlightened trappings in the profane realm. And it is
just that, friends; any place that is spiritually unhealthy is

not a good place, and it can be death's very house.

All of this posturing leads up to my saying that this step is a simple axiom for right living. The right concept of god or gods is the magic and love of the world, of the universe, and right spiritualism is the means by which we enhance and enrich our conscious contact with the love, peace, grace, beauty, magic, and light that is spirit. Despite my progressive theosophical definitions on these pages, of love and light and magical cognitive uplinks, and bunnies riding unicorns and fantastic things like that, one can nevertheless still do it the old-fashioned way: just pray out loud, when you have some time alone, or with friends if you have any. Lecture god, if you must. It is infinitely better than not at all starting a contemplative path. Or just cross your legs, sit, and listen to the stillness and peace that can be found in the universe. Spirit understands and forgives lecturers and listeners, and heals them both. Spirit is glad to have you, the world is spirit, you are part of it, and it happily accepts you at any time or stage.

When a person sees the singular importance of contributing positively to the improvement of the community and world around us, one realizes the importance of getting up and walking again, to incorporate and enfranchise or re-incorporate and re-enfranchise. With that, a person can effectively quit worshiping lower powers such as poisons like alcohol or other narcotics, and generally avoid the patterns of addiction that are paths to destruction and death that cloud the mind, harm the body, and kill the spirit.

Step Twelve

Having had a spiritual awakening as the result of these steps, we tried to carry this message to alcoholics, and practice these principals in all our affairs

Spirituality becomes a way of life. This step, as such, gets embarked upon as part of the natural order and progress of things. It is true in recovery, or a given spiritual path, or as with my case when the two are conflated, as they often are. A spiritual awakening as mentioned in step eleven illustrates the importance of contributing positively to the improvement of the community and world.

From step eight: "I am lucky to have been fished out. But to be fished out evidences a fisher, which indicates that there is another realm of historical contacts....this kind of watchfulness and awareness has become part of my grateful calling; I find that it requires a whole lot of praying for strangers."

These are some of the modes of living that I have learned from the examples set by people who historically have been involved with my case and rescuing me. I now pick up and carry on with the task. Having had a spiritual awakening, a person realizes that one of the most powerful vessels for spirit and love is through people, and everyone is capable.

Also, as mentioned in step nine, this recovery program is proven to be successful where others have failed, as a last resort. People who have made a full recovery are able to give back to the community using their valuable experience, expertise, and unique understanding and knowledge about addiction, addicts, and paths to recovery. There are many times and places in this world that are not sober environments, where sobriety is rare and precious. Any proven recovery program is an invaluable commodity not only to the particular target demographics that it directly serves, but also to the community at large.

As mentioned in step two, the program's application of the "higher power" idea, when introducing the concept of spirituality to new members (such as combative and/or confused drunk people who do not realize they are the victim of an extraordinary, transcendental disaster and that they are going to die a miserable death if they don't get help) is useful for anecdotal examination, through contrasting it with the notions of "lower power."

From step two: "Monotheism is perhaps best applied when one considers god as spirit or *anima mundi*, and the concept of god as spirit can be found in countless contexts. For example, I try to, at all times, be contemplatively mindful of the concept of god as spirit in some form or forms in some time or place, such as a star, a light, a piece of art, a river, a mountain, the sprawling galaxy above, a smile, a breeze, a laugh, a friendship, my own body, a flame, or among strangers. I also see the simple higher power and yet non-finite benevolence and worthiness in something as seemingly mundane as one hour of documented dry time where a person on the edge of relapse (or the grave, or what's the difference) can find safe asylum at a recovery meeting, for example. In a situation where one drink would further wet an already wet brain, bringing the body closer to death, the addict in recovery can surrender his worries and be in no danger of being further consumed for that hour. It may sound trite, but that is a kind of salvation. This is why, for example, jurists prescribe thirty recovery meetings in thirty days, or ninety in ninety for people on the edge of abyss."

Through these steps, there are numerous other examples of how one is naturally expected and inclined to, as a result of healing and spiritual awakening, carry the message of good news about hope and recovery to others who suffer from such addiction, and to apply such principals in all affairs, as we all should be doing, and should have been doing all along. It is the nature of life and the necessary behavior of people. It is like tending the soil. It can be hard work, but it is benevolent and rewarding, and is what sustains life and right living, and thus sustains us. Spirit empowers each of us in such a way that we become the open hand of god, if you will.

Marketplace Vigilance: Open Letters and Amici Curiae

The writings in this section are examples of how I established my own policies in response to problems in the business landscape.

They focus on issues in the marketplace which stand tall enough to regularly cause trouble or severely conflict with established ethical convictions in my field. I cannot go forward as a communicator without stopping to address certain issues on the path, and I have organized my personal and business operations to best address such hazards.

Now, whenever I encounter particularly egregious behavior, I have a known response protocol, and because the pen is a powerful tool and doing one's civic duty does everyone a favor, I encourage the same from everyone. Also, our enforcement agencies and offices are ours to execute, and this is how they are meant to be used. If you and I do not, then the wrong people must do; and, form tends to follow function.

The difficulties exampled here are often symptoms of bloated bureaucracies, whether in the public or private sphere. Such out-of-check cottage industries are, typically on a moral decline and they also effect a herd-like mentality that is hard on individualism and therefore on individualists.

Some of the typical problems illustrated in this section capture people not necessarily acting consciously in bad faith, but rather in their habitually leaning upon assumptions which they are conditioned to make in order to carry on their rote. Upon closer inspection, their functions may turn out to be not merit based whatsoever, and therefore wholly lacking. When one directly brings to bear a question of ethics, the response often reveals a kind of vacancy on the part of both the agent and its agency. Interestingly, in such circumstances that are devoid of affirmative purpose, the structure and function of the entire operation primarily serves to avoid responding to, if not altogether avoiding such an ethical question. Thereafter excepting the hodgepodge and transgression, the obfuscation is all that remains. This sort of business is rampant in the towns where I live.

On the other hand, there are still plenty of hustlers out there who are actively working in bad faith, and such actors are generally pretty stupid as a rule, but one does not have to be a genius to be a successful criminal, so watch out. Usually, the dumber and meaner is all the better, in fact. Such are better received and can work more efficiently amid non-thinking herds, and they thrive in situations where blind alleys are formed by vacancies in leadership and a lack of moral depth.

Also the whole situation is disgustingly aggravated by, among other things, the fact that most Americanos appear to be addicted to reds and blues, in the form of caffeine and alcohol, at least.

~CGB, January 22, 2015

Intellectual Property and Authors Rights

June 12, 2013

Texas Bar's Intellectual Property Section
Dallas, Texas;

Attorney General of Texas
Criminal Investigations Division
Special Investigations Unit
Houston/Austin, Texas;

Federal Bureau of Investigation
White Collar Crime/Intellectual Property Unit
Houston, Texas

This matter involves a question of authorship, copyright, intellectual tools, and definitions of "one's own work." The substantive issue is symptomatic of a more widespread dynamic, and I hope you find the information generally informative.

After college, I worked as a newspaper writer in southeast Arizona for four years, before returning in 2008 to Texas, where I have since worked in various support roles in the oil and gas industry. In the past five years, I have observed some widespread systematic dynamics that take advantage of creative talent to include scriveners such as myself, as one might expect in a large segment that contains many types of personalities and motives. I find myself now in a particular situation that illustrates this sort of organizational and institutional misbehavior, and I am only too happy to make this information available to any discovery effort or other investigation as needed.

My former employer [redacted] has retained an elaborate article which I composed about the use of unmanned aerial vehicles in the midstream and maritime sectors of the oil and gas industry. During the course of researching, writing, and interviewing for the article, I consulted numerous technical professionals. Sources included experts within the avionics and specialized support industries as well as regulatory officials. The work was done under the purview of my byline for eventual publication in one of the organization's various magazines.

After some stalling, the senior manager of magazines, who is the managing editor and my former supervisor, last week gave a position that the content is the organization's own intellectual property outright, refuses to return it to me, and prompted me in writing to make all further efforts toward relief through some court at law. Additionally, there was at various times during my twenty-eight months with this employer, some recurring oddities regarding the internal chain of custody of technical/journalistic articles that I composed. Also, about three months before my termination, the majority of the significant volume of content that I had produced along the way was pulled from web syndication, and the online archives were mothballed as the organization privatized (or capitalized, if you prefer) its digital content. With that, and excepting the articles which I wrote for the hard copy magazine editions, I have lost access to the volume of work samples that would properly account for my time and efforts with the organization, that leaves only the ex-supervisor who fired me in place to officially speak regarding my professional situation during those years.

I am encumbered by the stated position of the organization, because it does not satisfy the guarantees that I provided at my own risk under the auspice of my byline, to the sources in good faith during the project. The assurances were given by me on behalf of the project and the organization, with the understanding that the article would be published in a timely fashion, in exchange for the sources' cooperation and substantive input. Yes, I was working under the standard of the organization's logo, but the project was implemented entirely by me as the author and project manager, and strictly through my efforts at research and data collection to include soliciting, communicating with, and interviewing third party experts.

I submitted to the organization that author's rights supersede such an organizational claim in this instance. This is true particularly if the policy determination is not made in good faith, or where policy is misguided or intractable inasmuch as it is not reflective of the actual business landscape and notwithstanding fundamentally bad policy. I would not have a problem with the organization simply publishing the work in my absence, because it happens that I composed it while under its direct employ. However, that the organization has no intent to keep me honest is problematic for my professional reputation because I still operate using the same byline, moreover I still operate in the same capacity among the same industries and institutions.

Philosophically, the content of the project effectively demarcates a bright line beyond which the sources were willing to freely discuss the technologies featured in the article. So the organization has no applied argument, regarding the custody of trade secrets or otherwise embargoed content, to support its policy. Moreover, the specific content of the article is third party content.

The organization's presumed exclusive right to dispose of the written content in a fashion not guaranteed to my sources by me in my former capacity as one of its staff writers, as the project's liaison, and as an agent of the organization without enfranchising me in the dialog, is as patently illegitimate as would be the organization's presumption to negotiate with or settle procedurally with these sources on my behalf or regarding my staffed position after my leaving, which I presume the organization has likely attempted to do in order to secure blind alleys and to save face, and potentially even has done so at the cost of committing libel or slander. And if it has not attempted to do so, then blind alleys exist which, to the third party sources, would appear to have been personally created by me. Otherwise, the organization might argue that the final article is inferior work, but that is not an argument apropos the applied intellectual property policy in question, moreover the final article was valuable enough to me that I wish to retain it.

As an author, content creator, publisher, producer, business owner, and communications professional, I am obligated to protest when I see individual or systematic abuses of, or harmful applications of, intellectual property policies that are relevant to my field of expertise. The former employer's behavior in this instance has no logical grounds, amounts to nothing more than corporate-grade bullying of an individual, and is unacceptable. It is important to qualify that a working writer such as myself (who has a good reputation and a sizable published body of work) is an institution of a kind in his or her own right. I am incorporated, in fact, but I was a direct hire during my time with this organization.

In the marketplace, I apply intellectual tools, business approaches, and a professional reputation, which I have intently and painstakingly developed over the years. As an individual I simply do not release governing power over creative content to dead-handed machines, paper tools, bureaucracies, or compartmentalized vacuums, but in this instance, the authority has been wrestled from me, and wrongly so. Practically, such intellectual tools are part of a process flow which, amid not just a project but a career, must be respected, or be lost as a resource to the offending marketplace.

If my overall efforts were conducted in bad faith, then I would have no standing in this argument. And if I thought the policy was fair, moral, ethical, or right-minded, I would not suspect unethical, immoral, or criminal behavior nor would I be seeking relief. It is a simple contract issue, really. Intractable contracts are moot. Simply put, I did the work and I brokered the article content using my own intellectual tools, and incurred the business risk exposure, and ultimately, there is no good reason why the organization cannot cough up the article. Therefore, I am not inclined to remain in the position of professional liability where the organization's applied policy, in a fashion that I perceive to be in bad faith, has deposited me. For me to allow this to occur without seeking relief or reform only enables such abuses to continue and flourish.

In this instance, I think the policy was inspired at a personal or personality level, but it nevertheless occurred in an environment where such behavior is ubiquitous, and its prevalence is part of the problem. I was fired after twenty-eight months of employment with the organization, the majority of which time I endured significant animosity from my supervisor, whose decision to terminate seems to have been largely if not entirely based on his evident personal prejudice against me, that I documented in a formal written complaint to the organization's personnel office. If there may be any historical lack of performance on my part during the time of my employment, I would attribute it entirely to the negatively charged environment created and sustained by the supervisor. This negative interpersonal situation was not for any lack of effort toward amity on my part. However, my significant substantive concern herewith exists with the false intellectual property claim, and also to some degree with the anachronisms among the organization's internal custody-of-content methods (e.g. editorial copy flow), whereby the management is too busy screwing around between lunch and cubicles to actually audit the integrity of its internal forensic policies. So, this is not an EEOC complaint as such, although I believe there is also a worthwhile argument therewith. Again, I would be happy to further discuss this information as it may be determined to be timely or useful.

Verily,
Chris G. Braswell
Houston, Texas

Wireless Telecomm Marketing: Fair Warning

May 15, 2013

Attorney General of Texas
Criminal Investigations Division
Special Investigations Unit
Houston/Austin, Texas;

Federal Bureau of Investigation
White Collar Crime Division
Mass Marketing Fraud / Money Laundering Units
Houston, Texas

On the morning of May 16, 2013, I telephoned customer support for wireless communications company "Sprint" at [redacted], in order to temporarily downgrade my data and cellular telephony service package to a less expensive schedule. I requested that my service package be temporarily downgraded from the current rate of $121.21 per month to the least expensive version, at 200 minutes per month and without data service. I have done this before with the same company, however, the agent indicated that such service packages are no longer available for users of "smart phones." I concluded the phone call, and called again to attempt the same transaction through a different clerk, but received the same response.

Then I visited the company's nearest physical franchise location, at the corner of Westheimer Road and Kirkwood in the Westchase District of Houston. I made the same request, and explained that I had been granted one similar in 2010. I was instructed that "policy has changed since that time." I asked if my existing service package would allow for the provision of a new piece of hardware to accommodate their policy. The answer was no.

I informed the staff that I had some philosophical reserves about my request for a downgrade becoming an equipment upgrade purchase, but that I would consider the purchase of an inexpensive phone equipped only for cellular service and not data service, in order to retain my familiar phone number and Arizona area code, which I have had since I began my first contract with the company in 2004. I was informed that the least expensive piece of hardware in the store for such a purpose was about $290.

They suggested that I go to a nearby store to find a less expensive phone, which I attempted. It seemed clear that they were baiting me, since any phone I purchased from competitor stores in the area would not have Sprint firmware and therefore wouldn't be configured for Sprint wireless service. At the nearby "Verizon" store at the corner of Westheimer and Kirkwood, I was informed that its phones were of similar price, and furthermore would require a Verizon contract to function properly because of firmware installed on the devices it sells. Incidentally, the Verizon store smelled strongly of liquor (it was about 9:45 in the morning), which is a typical consequence of all of the illicit after-hours activity that goes on inside the confines of various light-business-zoned locations in the Westchase District. The clerk told me that the smell was "popcorn," and informed me that I might check across the street at the "ATT" wireless service center, which he said provides inexpensive wireless telephones that do not require a corporate contract.

[Editor's note: this situation has never been resolved. The technology is there, but the cottage industry surrounding them makes their use prohibitive. I have been using inexpensive, limited-function, pay-as-you-go wireless devices since this day, nearly two years ago, and I am

Personnel at the ATT location across the street said their phones were also not configurable to work properly with any other service other than its own, but the staff did provide me with a pre-pay type of wireless account involving a $35 start-up fee and at a rate of $50/month. Notably, the ATT store was clean, smelled normal, well lit, and had an armed Houston Police Department officer posted inside.

I returned to the Sprint store and told the staff that I wished to terminate my service contract. I was handed a land line telephone at the front end of the store, and in about one minute, a man named Robert picked up the line, requesting the reason for my call. I told him the story about my request for a temporary downgrade, which I had been granted several years prior. I explained that the data stream on my smart phone, which I owned, could be simply toggled on and off by the end user from the unit itself, but that I was still being asked to purchase a new telephone valued at about $290. Robert agreed to terminate my service, and waive the current month's payment cycle, which he indicated had begun "yesterday" (May 15). He further indicated that Sprint would fine me in the amount of $320, at which time all of the store's staff, which had gathered around a desk back at the far end of the store, burst out into a peal of laughter. I asked the man to explain the reason for fine, and he answered, "You do not want to pay your bill because you said it is too expensive, and so you are prematurely terminating your account, which is a breach of contract."

My approximate response: "No, I asked for a temporary service downgrade, which you will not grant me without the purchase of a new $290 piece of equipment and creation of a new contract. You can't have it both ways. I will not purchase a new piece of equipment, when I am holding one that does the same thing by its very design (referencing the data toggle button on the user interface)."

I explained that 1) when the contract that I have underwritten becomes so grandiose that I can no longer receive the basic wireless telephony service which was the whole reason for my business with Sprint, and, 2) when the technology to toggle the data service is apparent and already accessible to both the end user and the service provider, then the contract is out of step with the realities of the market environment and therefore unenforceable, fines and all.

I also inquired regarding how "Apple," the manufacturer of the equipment which I was currently using, might view the Sprint policy.

As our telephone conversation ended, the man terminated my Sprint account, and I inquired regarding whether he was in contact with me from a foreign country or a state, territory, or protectorate of the United States; to which he responded that he was in the United States. I asked him to reveal to me in what city or state he was in contact with me from, which he refused to answer three times. I asked him if he and I happened to be in same Sprint store at that very moment, and he declined to answer that question as well. I requested an incident number of reference in order to file this complaint, which he gave me [redacted] and I asked for his name, which is when he gave me the first name, although he refused to give me a last name or employee identifier.

After concluding the telephone conversation with him I walked over to the main desk in the back of the store, where the personnel still remained gathered after they had initially collected there when my telephone conversation had begun up at the front of the store. I asked a shaved-headed white male at the counter if he was the manager, and he said he was a manager. I asked him his name, which he provided. I asked him the specific name of the franchise at that location, and he said its name is Western Talk LLC. I inquired regarding the ownership of Western Talk since he said it was a limited liability company, and he refused to answer the question several times. At that point, a second Sprint staff member, a man with long, pulled back auburn hair, indicated that they were not obligated nor compelled to answer my question regarding who owns the franchise because it is a privately held company. I suggested that although it may or may not be privately held, the entity is still conducting business with a public currency in an open market, in a right of way open to the public, and as such is presumably attempting to operate in good faith, with auditable books, and that he should be forthwith to valuable clients regarding store information.

He did not respond. I asked him if he was a manager. He also said yes. I asked him his name. He said his name was "Robert Template." At that point the other man instructed Robert Template to refrain from talking to me any further.

The other man then gave me a business card, bearing a Sprint corporate logo, an assistant store manager's name, address, phone numbers, e-mail, and he also gave me an additional phone number which I wrote on the back of the card [all redacted].

So, my suspicion is that Mr. "Template" of the "call center" was also one of the several in-store assistant managers. The staff is so cavalier in their abuse of Sprint patrons and what must undoubtedly be their misrepresentation of the firm's corporate standard, that they felt comfortable enough to laugh right out loud about it while in the act of the offense, without regard for my clear awareness of it. Such a hive of "assistant managers" yet without any actual responsible administrator at hand, is a configuration that I have come to understand is widespread and commonly encountered among in-bad-faith operations, both in terms of management and accounting.

I do not believe my action to be a breach of contract, rather, I understand it to be 1) my evasion of abuse; incidental to 2) the substantive failure of the contract to provide reasonable conformance with the extant technology which it was created to govern. In light of the particular functionality of the device, which I did originally purchase outright from Sprint at the outset of the agreement in question, the contract is unenforceable.

When I returned home, I paid off the remaining $121.21 balance on the account, and though I have not received any bill of goods regarding the fine as threatened, I do consider it to be a harsh and illegitimate assessment. I would be happy to further discuss this matter and accommodate any investigation.

Verily,
Chris G. Braswell
Houston, Texas

Wireless Telecomm Marketing: Help Desk

May 27, 2013

Robert J. Evola
Bradley M. Lakin
St. Louis, Mo.

Anthony Vozzolo, J.D.
Faruqi Law
New York, N.Y.

Scott A. George
SeegerWeiss LLP
1515 Market Street No. 1380
Philadelphia, Penn.

I am a journalist and editor, currently doing business in the Houston, Texas area. Over the years, I have observed various antagonistic relationships between wireless telecommunications marketing franchises and their clients, but I witnessed a situation so grand on May 16, 2013, that I composed criminal complaints.

Seeking due process, I filed the attached report with the Texas Attorney General. Furthermore, as I searched about for any ongoing civil class action lawsuits that are germane and timely with respect to the information I've attached herein, I found *Larson v. ATT Mobility [Nos. 10-1285/1477/1486/1587]*, having been remanded to the lower court last summer ("Because the District Court did not adequately protect the rights of absent class members, we will vacate its order and remand the matter for further proceedings," according to: (www.ca3.uscourts.gov/opinarch/101285p.pdf).

With that, insofar as you may make use of my information and inasmuch as there is active discovery at hand today, I am only too happy to provide this report, to you and to your colleagues on the case. I am available as needed whenever you may have any further questions for me, or suggestions as to who otherwise might find this information useful.

Verily,
Chris G. Braswell
Houston, Texas

Wireless Telecomm Marketing: Direct Approach

June 17, 2013

Dear Sprint-Nextel,

Enclosed in this parcel is a copy of the criminal complaint I filed at the office of the Attorney General of Texas, in Austin, Texas, on 16 May 2013, regarding corporate Sprint-Nextel and Western Talk LLC doing business as Sprint Store By Western Talk at 8104 Southwest Freeway, Ste. A, Houston, Texas, 77074.

I also provided the same document to various agents involved with the civil litigation related to *Larson et al V. ATT Mobility et al, (U.S. Third Circuit Court of Appeals, 10-1285/1477/1486/1587)* to include Scott A. George of Seeger Weiss LLP in Philadelphia, Anthony Vozzolo of Faruqi & Faruqi, LLP in New York, and Robert Evola of SL Chapman LLC in St. Louis. The case was remanded to the lower court last summer, pending the consideration of absent class members.

I was assessed an early termination fee for alleged violation of contract. The reason I went to the store location was to temporarily reduce the scope of my service, for which I have contracted with Sprint for 10 years in multiple states and have never even been tardy with a payment. This particular request is one I have made from Sprint and been granted previously, and the Apple Inc.-brand wireless smart phone readily provides a toggle for the user to shut-off all data except telephony. However, I was instructed that rather than using the data toggle on the hardware, I would have to purchase a new unit and open a new contract to effect such a temporary reduction of service.

Such a "user agreement" is simply not in

conformance with the extant technology. I would view the policy differently if I were renting the device, rather than having purchased it from Sprint.

The store staff thought it was god damn funny. They were abusive and disrespectful, and together laughed at me and my frustration quite heartily. I terminated all of my association with Sprint and any and all of its affiliates on that day, walked across the street, and opened a pay-as-you-go account with a common carrier for half the cost. I suffered extreme diarrhea beginning a few hours later, which lasted several days, and having spent many years working in the restaurant industry, I do not place the store staff outside of suspicion regarding that particular issue either, unfortunately.

When a policy goes so far afield as to not facilitate the service of the provider's original intent nor the customer or business partner's original reason for involvement, and/or when a policy is substantively in conflict with the extant technology which was fundamental to the origination of the agreement, then the policy is intractable and cannot stand on its own merit. In awaiting relief from this sort of very commonplace road-agent practice among the communications marketing segment, I am put upon to ask corporate Sprint-Nextel to stand down from its "early termination fee" of two hundred ninety six dollars and twenty cents, at the very least, and among numerous other suggestions about your continuing to operate in this marketplace segment.

Verily,
Chris G. Braswell
Houston, Texas

Wireless Telecommunications Marketing: Third Party

Sent To Apple (availing no reply)

I recently ended an agreement with Sprint-Nextel. After requesting a temporary reduction in service scope, the agents said such an option was precluded for their Iphone users, and that I must purchase a new device and contract. I believed the policy to be at odds with the technology in hand, because the device allows its user simply to toggle wireless data on and off (as can Sprint-Nextel, which is the marketing end of the service provider, do easily likewise). I filed a detailed legal brief of the matter to civil and criminal investigators; corporate has since offered to waive its early termination fee in exchange for my return of the device. But, I ask of Apple's procedural preference before I give it back. Shall I return it or do you want it? I am also happy to provide Apple the documentation given to the FBI, to the Texas Attorney General, and to private attorneys involved in civil class action discovery.

Point-of-Sale Digital Accounting Fraud

June 28, 2013

Attorney General of Texas
Criminal Investigations Division
Special Investigations Unit
Houston/Austin, Texas

Federal Bureau of Investigation
White Collar Crime Division
Financial Institution Fraud / Asset Forfeiture / Money
Laundering Units
Houston, Texas

In late December 2012, the after-school transportation and daycare program at Grace Presbyterian Church in Houston, Texas, fired its department head on short notice and unexpectedly announced that it would no longer provide after-school service to our family. I began looking for immediate alternatives to cover the second half of the school year, once classes were to resume in January 2013.

I selected Samurai Karate Dojo at Dairy Ashford Street and Briar Forest Drive for its proximity to my son's school, its relative affordability, its clean and well-kept appearance, and the evident competency of its athletic / martial arts leadership for my son, who is six years of age and has taken strongly to a martial arts path for more than two years now.

The payment agreement between me and the Dojo was stipulated to involve automatic charges from my Wells Fargo checking account twice per month, plus initial fees. However, several times, the amount was struck from the account, after which the real-time online statement balance would reflect the charge, but then within the same business day the charge would disappear and the balance would reflect that of prior to the charge. Then the transaction would appear again to have processed following another period of one to three business days. This happened at least twice. All of the final transactions executed are still visible in the keyword-queried archive of transactions through my online account portal, a copy of which I have included. What is not evident in the online account history nor in the hardcopy bank statements, is a record of the incidences of the transactions being executed and subsequently rescinded before posting again and staying posted.

These sorts of digital "double charge" or "double hit" incidents are a key vector for black-market economies where such activity can be a formidable source of capital liquidity and a wide egress for shadow markets related to identity theft and digital banking fraud. This sort of activity is indicative of specific crimes which debase the currency.

I witness these "double hits" somewhat regularly, such as when a vendor clerk at a physical location says, "could you swipe your card again, it did not go through." This occurs frequently (at gas stations, grocery stores, etc.), and most recently to me this month, 14 June, in the Whole Foods Market franchise at Waugh Drive and West Dallas Street. The receipt for that grocery transaction is also included with this letter. It occurs frequently at automated gas pumps also, to name another good example. This particular mechanism can be engineered to occur even if the point-of-sale clerk is not involved, but I suspect that they usually are.

They may not be stealing from me individually, but in any case it destroys the efficacy of one of my strongest executable market tools, which is far worse and denotes a larger crime-victim demographic. If a clerk (or a clandestinely implemented protocol) can bank $10,000 out of nowhere by merely ghosting my buyer's identity with one flip of the wrist, it removes the market's incentive to accommodate me.

Again, more broadly speaking, the local personnel may not be the actor. It can be a technological agent, e.g., a computer system hack of malicious/clandestine script on the vendor's network, and/or it could be occurring within the banking institution's rights-of-way such as being associated with a card account number. Usually, though, the point of sale staff seems to be aware of it.

With respect to the situation at Samurai Karate Dojo, I suspect that responsible parties would be nearest the billing entity, although it is still not clear to me what entity was actually executing the payment transactions, or whether it was the service provider itself. On the part of corporate Wells Fargo or any of its widely distributed franchises, there is also the potential for collusion either at the employee or policy level.

The woman with whom I maintained dialog and entered the payment-for-service agreement with the Dojo functions as its office manager. The business' owner did not deal directly with point-of-sale interaction and he seemed to be largely focused, task-wise and ethically, on the center's training and curriculum rather than the bookkeeping or front-end office management aspects of the business, although I did briefly mention to him my concerns, regarding idiosyncrasies with the billing protocol, during a private, closed-door visit to his office one afternoon. Still, it could be a good-cop-bad-cop scenario in play.

Please find the attached list of historical transactions with Samurai Karate Dojo from my checking account, reflecting the charges that were terminally processed. In addition to reasons of general marketplace vigilance, and although on its surface these situations did not technically cost me any extra individually, it did expose me to at least twice the risk for overdraft fees, which is one of several reasons why I generally object to agreements involving automatic charges on my checking account. I was informed by the office manager at the outset that I did not have any other option for payment. She verbally detailed at that time that a third-party collection agency, about which she was reticent to provide further detailed information, handled all the business' payment transactions.

I appreciate your time in reviewing the contents of this document, and I would be happy to discuss this information further, inasmuch as it may serve any criminal or civil investigations into this or similar matters.

Verily,
Chris G. Braswell
Houston, Texas

Back Billing

July 9, 2013

Attorney General of Texas
Criminal Investigations Division
Special Investigations Unit
Houston/Austin, Texas;

Federal Bureau of Investigation
White Collar Crime Division
Corporate Accounting Fraud / Identity Theft Units
Houston, Texas

Having recently moved my family to a new rental address, I used the transition as an opportunity to eliminate redundancies and deficiencies in service among various residential/home-office utility and communications services agreements.

One change has been the termination of a broadband cable Internet service agreement with Comcast Corporation [account number redacted]. In mid-May, I telephoned the number [redacted] provided on the Comcast bills, requesting that the service be terminated by the end the month, which was the last day of the lease agreement at our former residential address in west Houston. The Comcast agent on the line said May 21 marked the end of the billing cycle, and he said to terminate service on that date would avoid charges for the subsequent monthly cycle. The 21st was a few days before our move date, but it was close enough, so I agreed. I also inquired regarding how to return the Comcast-issued modem in my possession, and whether it was possible to do so by postal mail.

The following Friday, May 24, was moving day, and also the day that all utility and communications services were implemented at our new address in north Houston.

More-competitively priced DSL network service from Houston-based Oplink began at the new residence on this day, and ourselves and all of our belongings, including our household communications equipment, were permanently relocated from our previous residence by then.

When Comcast's monthly billing cycle came around for June, I received a bill for $76.36, for the service period from May 22 through June 21, stipulating payment due by June 6. I again telephoned the number provided on the bill. I conversed with a different person who indicated that the problem was likely the result of the bill having been sent before the corporation's records were updated regarding my account, and that it would be fine if I just ignored the bill, because the company's records would, in due time, be corrected to reflect the appropriate account termination date. This I did, and I thanked her for the helpful information, although I have heard such statements before and it has never turned out to have been an accurate assessment of the situation. I also asked after any physical Comcast locations in my new neighborhood where I could drop off the modem.

Today, July 9, 2013, I got another bill from the company, the front of which itemizes the mis-assessed and still-uncorrected previous balance of $76.36 in a "monthly statement summary." The total outstanding balance is listed on the front of the bill as $86.60 with payment due by July 21. The new charges summary itemizes a "partial month charges and credits" item for a credit of -(74.34); an "other charges and credits" charge of $89.48; and a "tax/surcharge/fee" credit of -(4.90); with these amounting to the "new charges" balance of $10.24.

On the back of the bill I found three more itemized charge/credit lists. The first list on the back is the aforementioned "partial month charges and credits." The second list on the back of the bill, "other charges and credits," lists a charge of $90 assessed on July 1 for unreturned equipment, and noting that all equipment must be returned to the company to have the related charges removed from my account, which I am happy to comply with. The other item is a -(0.52) credit for a fee assessed to its customers by Comcast to compensate itself for taxes that are apparently imposed by the state of Texas upon the Pennsylvania-based corporation which processes its payments in Utah.

The third and final list on the back of the bill, "taxes, surcharges, and fees" reflects a credit of -(4.16) for "state and local sales tax" and a credit of -(0.74) for "Montgomery CO Emergency Serv Dist. 9" (note, the service address was in a Harris County, not Montgomery County).

Also today, after receiving the bill, I again telephoned the service number provided on the Comcast bill, and talked with "[redacted]" who told me his employee number is [redacted], and that his employee telephone extension is [redacted].

I explained to him the history of the termination of my former Comcast account and the erroneous charges from the period of 5/21-6/21. I again requested that the corporation's records be corrected to reflect that I am no longer a customer, and that the outstanding balance of $76.36, stemming from the errant billing, be reconciled to zero on the company's books, and that the previous account in my name be updated to reflect the actual service termination date.

The agent said that when I returned the modem, all charges on my account would be zeroed out, and then I would quit receiving bills from Comcast. It is therein that I see a potential problem with the company's bookkeeping that causes me to suspect that I or my peers in the marketplace are the victims of attempted/systematic accounting fraud.

I assured the agent that I would now return the modem promptly, and wait to see if next month's bill (if I receive one) reflects a zero balance. But I also said that I am not convinced that the effort of corporate Comcast, its billing department, or its local franchise(s) or staff are in conformance with the law as it relates to privacy and accounting fraud. Had I not retained the modem until it was clear that the company had closed its book on me, I would not have seen this apparent liability that was made to appear to be the result of incompetent accounting methods.

Comcast is "holding the door open," so to speak, by its incorrectly assessed service/billing period. It raises the question of what prevents the company from leaving an outstanding balance on a book in the amount of a month's worth of service for all of its outbound customers. Or how about ten years for all of its outbound customers who do not catch them doing it? This corporate mechanism could spoof entire lifetimes of service contracts for entire community populations and the specific victims would never know of, much less be apt to isolate or hem in the writ large vector. Perhaps widespread activity of this nature is why I am a blue chip driver with great credit, but nevertheless I am nickeled and dimed severely at every turn, and discriminated against as a certain class of naïve, over-ethical, "know-nothing" market operator.

But the marketplace at large knows it. Such wholesale bar theft, which gets a toehold through jackal-like abuse of the concept of implied consent, through broadly-tailored definitions of corporate influence and its rights of way, is why there are so many thousands of people with no functional education and no applied vocation who are driving around Houston in expensive automobiles wielding military-grade telecommunications equipment. One does not need to be literate to successfully commit fraud when he or she has a logistical war hammer in one hand and an organized chokehold on the local purse with the other. And at the corporate level, I am not here to, voluntarily or otherwise, underwrite Comcast or its shareholders using paper tools or any other legalistic means. They did not ask, so it is a taking that I did not authorize, and that is against the law of the land.

Even if the company does actually purge the wrongly assessed charge, it will not correct the fact that it did establish a debt fund at the expense of a non-existent account, which now and always will have had a month's worth of my name on it as the principal, regardless of its legitimacy. So as far as I know, everywhere except in my mind, that account can be thought of as actualized.

That amounts to a lot of philosophical dollars. No matter what happens now, it is a fact that a fund was bonded with myself as the unwilling guarantor. And now that my suspicion has been evoked regarding the company's accounting practices and moral compass, how am I to audit the company once I quit receiving "bills" from them, which by this point, I am not even supposed to be getting in the first place? Their foot is already in the door. There is a strong argument that I should not only conduct a private investigation regarding this particular situation, but also apply such a forensic policy in all my business activities, and with implications about the nature of my situation as a marketplace operator.

That is the crux of this complaint. Even if it is just sloppy accounting and not intentionally fraudulent accounting, in any case it creates a blind alley for fraud.

Such an overarching trend in the marketplace would seem to be forensically linked to more widespread situations of this general nature. In any case, the company's clerical position seems to be far off-the-mark in terms of prudent accounting in good faith.

Furthermore, does the statement made by the corporate agent represent a sound ethical position on the part of the company he represents? Essentially, he indicates that all of the accounting processes between Comcast and myself, including the suspicious retroactive formatting and erroneous billing charges, will all simply just "go away" once I deliver the modem. Regarding that, I plan to take the modem in tomorrow.

I have long suspected that the return of the hardware to a physical location was part of the fraudulent scheme, perhaps being a critical aspect for an information hand-off or other tacit collaboration among unknown third parties operating in bad faith. The terminal at the return location will certainly have access to an online record-keeping system which contains my billing information.

This sort of accounting activity is evidently commonplace. Perhaps there needs to be tort reform to protect against consumer accounting fraud, which negatively affects the business environment and erodes the value systems involved. In the same breath that I mention tort reform, however, I realize that such rulemaking is moot in light of the fact that it is already illegal to lie, cheat, and steal. In any case, in addition to enforcement of civil law, I hope this example is firm enough to provide teeth for any related criminal investigations, because criminal prosecution sets a precedent too.

I am looking for some way to protect myself and my peers in business from such hazards, and one way I know to do that is by writing letters like this. If I do not make an appropriate effort to maintain legitimacy and integrity within the sphere of my own vocation, as a communications and media professional, consultant, author, and publisher, then it reflects poorly upon my own competence.

Also, I would just briefly mention that, if Comcast is insisting on providing people with end-use modems (and it does insist) in order to represent itself in the marketplace as a common-carrier infrastructure provider, for lack of any other actual ownership of public rights of way, then that is an insult to anyone who has ever dug a utility line.

Thank you for taking the time to read this information, and I would be happy to elaborate and assist in any investigation efforts herewith or similar, criminal or civil. A copy of the June 2013 and July 2013 bills sent to me by the company (front and back), are attached to this letter.

Verily,
Chris G. Braswell
Houston, Texas

Progressive Marketing and Accounting Fraud

October 31, 2013

Attorney General of Texas
Criminal Investigations Division
Special Investigations Unit
Houston/Austin, Texas;

Federal Bureau of Investigation
White Collar Crime Division
Financial Institution Fraud and Failures
Mass Marketing Fraud
Houston, Texas

About 8:30 on the morning of October 30, I logged in to my online checking account balance (printed document attached), to discover a pending transaction in the amount of $25, with the description "CHKCARDB&N MEMBERSHIP NEW YOR NYUS." Though I have not shopped at any Barnes & Noble bookstore franchise at all in recent months, I supposed that this was the organization signified by "B&N," which fraud investigators at my banking institution confirmed later that morning.

As a magazine editor and an author, I have an interest in books and bookstores, and late last year after purchasing all holiday seasonal gifts in one stop at Barnes & Noble, I was offered and accepted a corporate discount card to take advantage of the discount on the purchase. It was made clear to me by the clerk at the time, that the card did not denote a line of credit. If it had, I would have declined the discount card, which in itself is a marketing vector that creates exposure to all sorts of liabilities that I typically try to avoid anyway.

Yesterday's transaction was unauthorized and it is an

example of a common fraud vector, that is by way of marketing operations' misuse of people's personal and consumer data. This instance was flagrant because the clerk who provided the discount card explicitly stated that it was not a line of credit nor any other type of fund.

As a publisher and an author, I like bookstores. But if I or my business presence is to be used as an underwriter for corporate Barnes & Noble, not only do I need to be made aware of it beforehand, but also I must be involved in the negotiation of such an agreement, even if it is a gift. Ironically, I have since published a novel that is available through the bookstore's website, further illustrating why I need to be involved with corporate policy if it is going to directly involve my individual power of the purse.

Generally speaking, this sort of "auto-renewal" contrivance, in its seemingly small-dollar amount, even when occurring in the context of usurious credit funds, can be overlooked by a typical consumer or shopper, and given the benefit of the doubt as a legitimate charge. Operators in bad faith rely on such apathy. As a working journalist who is frequently conducting investigations into this sort of activity, however, I am potentially quicker to identify and act upon it. Many people do not react as aggressively, and so this sort of behavior by marketers is tacitly encouraged in the marketplace.

I have long suspected other sorts of unethical behavior stemming from discount cards, and I usually avoid them. Such cards, with their childish tit-for-tat affectations under the guise of "creative marketing," are no more than a way to collect, store, transact, track, and otherwise act upon personal information. Also, I have reason to believe that black books are kept by certain marketers who illicitly quantify and report such discount cards as lines of credit, or worse, they "sell" the identities of targeted consumers on a black market. Many such marketing agents, venues, or point-of-sale personnel are far less overt in their data collection and subsequent handling of it.

A short time later on the same morning, I telephoned the corporate Wells Fargo fraud reporting line [redacted] from my home office land-line telephone, reaching service clerk [redacted]. I explained the situation, and she said that in order to file a claim, my Wells Fargo credit/debit card and number had to be closed, and a new card and card number had to be issued. I stated to her that such policy seemed to be wrongheaded, forensically, in light of the accounting parameters necessary for such digital transactions to have occurred in the first place. The bank's decision here was an example of an institutional policy that encourages a culture of ethical nonaccountability and creates a banking operation that is more difficult to investigate or audit. It also would seem to invite unethical people or groups of people into the banking industry.

As a community member and a businessman, I appreciate the multiple roles of the dollar as they relate to me, and each time I use it I am mindful and watchful of the transaction, in case of events such as this. In very real ways, encountering an instance of apparent fraud is a good thing inasmuch as it can now be investigated and resolved. In every transaction that I make, particularly considering the digital nature of check card transactions, I am aware of the liability, but I am also technologically awake, and I am always happy to contribute to the day-to-day oversight of the marketplace.

It is operationally cumbersome for me to have to replace the card and the number, but what is more important is that replacing the card and the number does not change the odds of it happening again. It is a lateral (at best) procedural step with no saving grace. It exposes me to far wider liability of identity theft because I will no longer be able to administrate and monitor the card as it was quantified, and I am not convinced at all that corporate Wells Fargo is able to do so. While I willingly continue to incur the ongoing hazard of transacting digitally, to the benefit of the bank among other parties, the bank's policy creates a new blind alley whereby my former (and historically lengthy) transaction information could still be used for illegitimate activity, without my being privy to the record. Would-be defrauders and would-be point-of-sale transaction administrators cannot be necessarily counted on to report the use of the old card data. In their eyes, an apparently valid card is a valid card, and an apparent customer in good-faith is just that, and that is all they may be concerned about regardless of whether or not they are criminals.

The bank's policy opens up a blind alley, to me, and the marketplace, and exposes all legitimate operators to the added risk. I am supposed to take it upon faith that the bank's top-to-bottom corporate personnel are beyond reproach. However, investigators or financial consultants must well understand that much bank fraud occurs inside the organization, or between a party inside the organization and some external third party. The bank's policy to change the card number, from my perspective, is 1) a potential forensic shunt, 2) adds entropy to the circumstances of the incident, and 3) creates undue additional liability to multiple parties.

After hearing these points made, the agent interrupted to say that her supervisor wished to take over the phone call, and then came [redacted] on the line, to whom I reiterated the reason for the call and my position on the Wells Fargo policy in the matter. She confirmed my request to file an investigative claim and issued me a claim number. The supervisor said the bank policy could be found in the company's general corporate, and fraud protection disclosure documents on the bank's web site, but I could not immediately locate this governance on the web site. She gave me some additional clerical information, authorized the claim, and told me to expect by U.S. Mail a new card bearing a new number.

This woman was helpful and patient with me, and seemed to have a clear understanding of the points I was making. I informed her that I have had some previous complaints in recent months about some issues with Wells Fargo's fraud security, for example about institutional policy that allows for "double hit" third-party billing transactions, which create a fertile accounting environment for the spoofing of account balances, the black market cloning of digital funds, and outright theft of individuals' financial identity.

I reiterated to the bank agent that it is entirely my choice as a business owner and individual to be or not to be a Wells Fargo customer, and that I am put upon adversely by its apparently incompetent, potentially unethical, technologically byzantine, and intellectually dishonest corporate policy. At least with the old card number, there was a predictive trend regarding my behavior in the marketplace, which would seem to make it easier for my banking agent to interdict fraud attempts targeting or related to my account. It is preposterous for the bank to act as if there has been no fraud or fraud attempts with my previous card information, in the twenty-odd years that I have had the account. It is even more ridiculous for the bank to propose that changing the number will change anything among the criminal element, or otherwise improve the marketplace, or help me navigate that marketplace, or contribute to a solution for this particular issue.

The supervisor transferred me to a financial crime specialist [redacted] in Phoenix who read me a short questionnaire and briefed me regarding the weather out there.

I appreciate your time in reviewing the contents of this document, and I would be happy to discuss this information further, inasmuch as it may serve any criminal or civil investigations into this or other relevant matters now or at any time in the future.

Verily,
Chris G. Braswell
Houston, Texas

State Insurance Contractors: A Cottage Industry

December 4, 2013

Attorney General of Texas
Criminal Investigations Division
Special Investigations Unit
Houston/Austin, Texas

Federal Bureau of Investigation Houston Office
White Collar Crime Division
Public Corruption, Civil Rights, Counterintelligence
Department

On December 3, I called telephone number [redacted] listed on my son's insurance policy card, which was issued to me for health insurance coverage of a dependent, by the Texas health and human services office. As I and my family are moving to the greater Phoenix area this month, I had questions such as whether I must notify or whether I am required to withdraw from the program, and whether the policy will remain valid until the term ends in June 2014 and whether the policy would be accepted by out-of-state emergency responders and health care providers.

On the upper right-hand corner of the card (a copy of which is attached) reads the acronym "CHIP," which I supposed was in some way analogous to "Texas Children's Health Plan," which was also written on the card. However, after some conversation with the woman [redacted] on the line, I learned that, yes, CHIP denotes the state agency's welfare program in this instance (Children's Health Insurance Program), but that Texas Children's Health Plan is the business of the woman who had taken my call, and that the company is a state contractor.

I have a gut feeling that I may have been her only

client, as the insurance segment seems have proven itself to be a cottage industry of questionable moral turpitude. My suspicion was increased when she aggressively attempted to compel me to provide additional personal information to her "system" such as our future address. Giving due and explicit caveats about fraud and the right-to-know, I declined to provide her the information. At that, she reiterated that she did not represent the state, and that she was not the proper source to answer my questions. She referred me to the state's health and human services general switchboard number [redacted]. Both of the phone calls represented in this complaint are documented in the attached audio files.

So, the woman was mush-mouthed when coaxed into explicitly admitting that she was not an agent for the state of Texas, and she remained duplicitous even after finally admitting that hers was a for-profit organization. Generally, the massive insurance cottage industry includes operators who squat at the back door of not just organizations but individuals, and when you encounter them and ask them what they are doing or try to run them off, they obfuscate.

Next I telephoned the state agency and first talked with [redacted], who indicated that the policy would not be binding out of state, that I must formally withdraw, and that it takes up to thirty days to process a withdrawal. He first said that I should wait and set into motion the withdrawal process right before our move date. I expressed concern that his advice could result in a gap in my son's coverage of up to thirty days, and requested that he begin the formal process immediately, which he did.

After he set the process in motion, he said that I would be notified by mail after the coverage was terminated. I asked him to clarify if and how the calendar date for the termination of service would be communicated to me beforehand, and he said it would not be. I explained that such non-availability of time and date information does not meet and would never meet the typical expectations of any legitimate operator or client. We had a few words about how our government is a public contract that becomes functionally out of order when it does not properly serve its constituents. At that point, I asked for his and his administrator's identifying information, which he refused to provide, but said that he would transfer me to someone who was a supervisor and who would provide the info.

It may seem to be only a slight offense against me, but speaking in a more general sense, the agency's policy seems to be intentionally muddy in order to preserve the cottage industry that "profits" from the status of many of its beneficiaries, at the expense of the labor force or "tax base." Instead of conforming with the intent of the program, the policy has been bent to support a self-serving bureaucratic vocational caste, among an insurance industry that is widely known to be dubiously unethical.

He transferred me to the call center in Athens, Texas, he claimed, and I talked with [redacted], who said her agent number was [redacted]. She eventually informed me that she was not a supervisor, and she either could not or would not give me the information that I required in order to file a complaint. At that point, I realized the call center agents had become antagonistic. Subsequently, they did not receive my most gentle mannerisms for the remainder of the call. However, I tried to salvage the time as best as I could, within reason; they did get a lecture in civics, and for better or worse they were ultimately told where to go. She also refused to give me mailing addresses and supervisor names, and transferred me to [redacted], who said his agent number was [redacted], but he seemed also dangerously ill-informed regarding who his supervisor was, and regarding his role as an agent for, or official of, a public government.

Fundamentally, the agents' own general lack of understanding of their context in the marketplace at large reflects poorly upon whatever system(s) are incumbent to educate them about the philosophical importance of their roles. Either that or theirs is contrived ignorance.

So while this program is a welfare program, it does not operate outside of market factors. An agreement is intractable if it is out of step with market factors, like, for example, if it cannot be put on a business calendar. And just because something has a democratic mode does not mean it is legal or legitimate. While my minimum expectations for competence were not met, I still estimate that the state of Texas would have been politically willing and able to serve me here, but the various elements in place for the particular business segment in question were standing in the way.

The policy does nothing to help welfare recipients better integrate into the marketplace at large, and it sets a terrible example for management and ethics. It violates the egalitarian nature of American political philosophy, hearkens back to darker times, and it encourages class lodging as a way of life.

As usual, I am happy to comment or cooperate further on this issue or any similar investigation, as appropriate. Also, henceforth I will likely file all further communications with through the bureau in Phoenix.

Verily,
Chris G. Braswell

The Press and Public Rights of Way

4 February 2014

Rodney J. Ross
Policy Advisor
Arizona State Senate
1700 W. Washington
Phoenix AZ 85007

Mr. Ross,

I saw that the Yuma Desalination Plant was on the Senate Rules Committee agenda today at 1 o'clock, and as you know, I am working on an article about the facility and about Arizona water in general. I went down there to the meeting, just in case anyone might express any strong opinions or useful perspectives on the topic.

Of course, it soon became clear that the Senate Rules Committee is a lot less of a production than, say, the House Ways And Means Committee, and unfortunately I could not hear the conversation of the committee through the very low volume on the PA system in the room. As you probably know, Senate Caucus Room 1 is not a bench-style setup with a nave, it is a boardroom style arrangement that is less conducive to an audience. When I moved to sit closer (I anticipated the problem when I first arrived, and had asked and received permission from one of the pages to move closer if needed be), I was intercepted and detained by the head of security. Soon, the meeting adjourned, and I of course did not hear any of the committee dialogue.

I spoke with the young security chief for a few minutes, before I was shown the door and while I was being passively detained as his security staff presumably made determinations regarding whether or not to escalate my detention, during which time he indicated that I could always go pay for transcripts of such meetings, and also that I would be welcome to plug into the A/V port to better hear or record the content. I explained that I had only a notepad, and I also told him that, as a press agent and a citizen, I am privy to witness the meetings as they occur, and to maintain such an expectation.

There are two main reasons why our magazine keeps an office downtown, and one of them is the proximity to the seat of government. The gentleman was perfunctorily parliamentary in his demeanor and quite level in his disposition, nevertheless his paramilitary training was preeminent. His vocational hackles were up and the room knew it. His behavior was disappointingly aggressive. I was somewhat embarrassed because heads did turn as it was a fairly intimate setting. And of course, I missed the meeting.

I was wearing my press badge on a lanyard around my neck, freshly shaven clean, physically fit, and well groomed, with good teeth, dressed in a collegiate and reasonably tasteful, pressed, matching, business-casual ensemble with coat, tie, and suspenders, and I cooperated with him harmoniously, in showing my press pass and business cards upon request. Furthermore, I intentionally arrived about ten minutes early, so any and all technical adjustments or caveats or instructions or prejudices for me or for members of the press or the public could easily have been instructed during that time, as I was making adjustments and communicating with the security staff. I feel sure that it was just a general misunderstanding on the part of a rather young, partisan, mop-headed security agent in a navy sportcoat, but looking ahead, I simply wish to avoid any similar situation. The American citizenry does not have to govern itself from that building, or from any other specific or fixed location, and certainly will not if barred from it. In any case, I was made to feel errant *persona non grata* and treated like a pantaloon.

Last month, before the legislative session opened, I visited with building security personnel and provided my personal and business information as a member of the press, in order to avoid this sort of thing. While we cannot attend every hearing, our magazine has an editorial policy of maintaining a regular presence at the capitol, as journalists, out of respect for our system of self government and the electors.

Meanwhile, on the YPD article, I have now had helpful interviews with the Central Arizona Project, the Bureau of Reclamation, and NOAA. Again, I appreciate the previous response from your office regarding the YDP. If possible, please keep me apprised of any additional action related to the pending legislation or other relevant policy news.

Verily,
Chris G. Braswell
Phoenix, Ariz.

Organized Crime, Civil Rights, and Whistleblowing

July 7, 2014

Senator John McCain
United States Senate
241 Russell Senate Office Building
Washington, D.C. 20510

2201 East Camelback Road
Suite 115
Phoenix, Ariz. 85016

Dear Senator McCain,

I have consulted with two "practicing attorneys" in recent days about a complaint to be filed at the United States District Court for the District of Arizona, regarding the apparent unconstitutionality of the United States income tax. Neither attorneys have been interested, citing such reasons as 1) it would be viewed as a frivolous lawsuit by colleagues on the bar 2) the case would be "unwinnable" 3) the action would constitute a real threat to a complainant's person, family, and liberty, and 4) there is hearsay about high court apologetics for the income tax in question.

However, from my vantage, "winning" is not the primary object of such a filing; rather, the capital point is the proper and circumspect conduct of my own civic due diligence, the dereliction of which, in my view, is most certainly far more perilous to my (and my neighbors') states of liberty. Examples of what happens when people neglect their civic duty are everywhere. We exercise our rights to reinforce them, otherwise we risk losing our rights.

This particular argument is upstream of any position regarding the unconstitutionality of the Sixteenth Amendment. Rather, the United States Constitution, Article I Section VIII, ascribed to the United States Legislature the power of the purse. Therefore, the nation's rulemaking body has no need to use my labor as its mint. Nevertheless, by its doing so I am, in effect, held in bondage to a writ that has no enforceable value beyond its symbolism of Congressional fiat. It certainly has no value beyond my spirit and freedom and vocation, and such a dynamic violates the liberty of mind and body to which I am a legacy, as is affirmed by the Constitution.

You and I and all citizens must not forget that we are our government; that is why this situation is important to me and by the same logic, it is important to you. My perspective does matter because I come by it honestly and in good faith; to wit, that the Congress and/or the Treasury misunderstands its role, and/or, that a malefactor is acting out of ignorance and/or in bad faith on behalf of the Congress and/or the Treasury.

My best option for specific legalistic recourse available to me, in order to peaceably establish an historical record of my position, is not exactly clear in light of the fact that the attorneys with whom I've spoken are unwilling for me to hire them for their counsel regarding process. These attorneys were said to be the most appropriate points of contact regarding such matters among the local cottage industry surrounding the courts.

I suggest that a False Claims Act (31 U.S.C. §§ 3729–3733) complaint would be appropriate in construing that the local organization which is doing business as the Internal Revenue Service is, in effect, defrauding the United States government through its treatment of me in my own vested rights as a United States citizen, and that the Congress and the Treasury are being misinterpreted by the same offender or group of offenders.

Relief through the False Claims Act is apropos for my case, inasmuch as the incumbency of my naturally governing civil agency is not only affirmed by the Constitution as the law of the land, but specifically vested in the three branches of the federal government. There is a strong possibility that it would be the first such approach regarding the question of the Constitutionality of the federal income tax brought in the light of the False Claims Act. I certainly do not mind filing in pro se, and what is most important to me is that I place my position on the record with the clerk of the court for historical purposes.

Again, we are the government and as such, the dollar, like the federal courts system, or the Congress, or the Treasury is a construct of the government that was fundamentally set forth for us. Our government entities are not uncontrollable mysteries, nor are they only controllable by mob rule, regardless of what various local for-profit jurists or attorneys or legalists or their respective derelict fiscal caucuses recently have to say about the matter. And at such time that our agencies are no longer in conformance with the natural laws iterated by the Constitution, they can no longer be binding upon the citizenry.

I did pay the income tax for 2013, at a local location. As I emptied my pockets and removed my belt before I and my son walked through the body scanner, I observed that the armed guards who were working the door were all well groomed and their gray uniforms clean. I suppose the context makes them the armed guards of the Congress, or is that only the story as the tax collector would tell it? This is a very important distinction to make.

I remarked to the United States Army veteran (named

Alex) who received my check, that, for example, the transaction which was occurring at that moment would best be described as "Chris and Alex DBA the United States of America."

Regarding the incidental relevance of the Army, I feel certain that Old Sarge there at the desk would have a compelling opinion about liberty and the Constitution. I suppose I am glad he was there to take the check, rather than someone who could not accurately define their station as that of a bond agent. But the path for me to underwrite NETCOM and the Corps of Engineers, as it were, was in this case convoluted and circuitous, and upon reflection of my accidental audit, *prima facie* appears to be coerced.

In all instances where the concept of self government can be a simple as "Chris and Alex DBA the USA," then it must be. Otherwise, a situation of republicanism has broken down and the civil agency or governing authority is out of order.

I have always paid the federal payroll and income taxes, since I began bagging groceries at age fifteen. Now that it has come to my attention that the income tax is apparently a violation of my natural rights as a free man, an American, and a United States citizen, I am put upon to peaceably file a complaint in the proper venue or venues. I understand this to include filing with the clerk of the District Court (in addition to opening this dialog with a Congressional elector).

The only thing on my collection letter that said "United States" was the post mark. I have been a working journalist for fourteen years; today I am a pro bono public press agent and an investigative reporter. I must say that the financial collection note which I received, in concert with the signed letter from a local collections agent and an

IRS collections manual which anyone with five minutes of access to a computer and printer could produce in full, all amounts to an applied effort that is quite indistinguishable from various common mechanisms that I have encountered in the marketplace when I have conducted accounting and financial fraud investigations. With economic fraud, there is always a blind alley, there is always subterfuge, and there is always a lynch-pin agent (who is often ignorant of his or her own role in the operation). There is also often black market information transactions or leaks and there is always some seal, standard, corporate logo, or other symbolic letterhead used to facilitate, shield, or politically enable the crime. That is, fraudulent document letterheads never say, for example, "Fraud by Con Artist" or "Road Agent" or "Forger" or "Organized Criminal Enterprise" or "Train Robber."

At best, the process as it relates to me, appears to be at least partially privatized with respect to the collection process, and compartmentalized administratively in terms of accounting in such a way that effects a perpetual invasion of my privacy. Moreover, it is not only Constitutionally unfounded, but is also in explicit violation of the letter of the law. Although the local collections agent told me that no individual investigation regarding my person or activities had been assigned or conducted beyond the information which I volunteered, the overall process does not appear to have occurred in plain view.

Historically, I have filed forensic information related to fraud in the marketplace with the appropriate federal law enforcement agency departments for criminal complaints, and with state attorneys general for civil complaints. If I cannot find any support on this matter, I suppose I will just file this complaint with the FBI like I have often done in previous matters as an effort at due process. But I expect that I might find moral, political, and civil support to file a complaint at District Court, which may be the best venue for this effort. That is why I am compelled to share this situation with you, sir. I believe this to be a philosophically compelling issue, and also I see it as a critically important issue, even potentially emergent with respect to at-large justice and my or any individual's civic duty. Regardless of the exact path, it is important that I do something in my capacity as a scrivener, an investigator, and a patriot.

Most Faithfully, Respectfully, and Verily,

Chris G. Braswell
Consulting Editor
Braswell Communications
Palmaire Precinct
Arizona Legislative District 28
United States Congressional District 9
Phoenix, Ariz.

WTF Federal Income Tax

December 3, 2014

U.S. District Court for the District of Arizona
(Case Number 4:14-CV-02574-TUC-JAS)

Today, the dollar is a symbolic currency, in the sense that it has an idealogically based valuation rather than some commodity based standard such as gold.

The American lawmaking body is constitutionally ascribed with a "power of the purse," though it has no need to arbitrarily tax the domestic workforce for the purpose of appropriating capital. In the absence of such a standard as the nation's former gold-based mechanism, the contemporary domestic workforce fulfills its philosophical role in certain applications of the dollar simply by electing to make use of it, or to patronize the dollar, in the marketplace at large.

Weakening the fortitude of the economy by burdening the earning and spending power of the citizen workforce, and thus exposing it to the increased liabilities of instability, is not in the best interest of the government of the United States. The U.S. government is one and the same as the egalitarian citizenry in the explicit absence off a ruling class.

Rather, a congress can look to the Federal Reserve Bank as the financial entity to provide liquidity for the nation's treasury. It is not rational or practical to appropriate any arbitrary portion of the earnings of the citizenry, excepting a volunteer basis, and under no circumstance should it happen without there being a forensically transparent budget for any given individual citizen's assessment. The mandatory appropriation without cause, of a citizen's earnings by any agency doing business as a U.S. government agency at best represents a fundamental misapplication of the dollar as a tool and a misunderstanding of the dollar as a modern institution.

From my vantage, such disorientation regarding the rule of law in our federal system seems to be common. To correct what appears to be a widespread misunderstanding (or perhaps rather to interdict widespread propaganda) regarding the nature and intent of our system of national government, requires an understanding that, by its design, the federal system is one of the most localized forms of government that can exist. Federalism in its pure form is a system of completely decentralized national government best applied for geographically large countries.

It follows that federal funding should be predominately if not entirely a concern for funding local infrastructure and operations. Beyond those needs, if there is any surplus, then the local constituency can make its democratic determinations regarding whether or not there is cause to ship its common wealth out of state or otherwise beyond the local area of its primary governing authority.

Someone who pays a federal income tax should be able to easily and locally review, in person, the majority of, if not all of one's tax dollar investments in his or her community. Such is the nature of federal agency; whether it is the special agent in charge at the local FBI office, one's neighborhood postmaster, or the district attorney, federal agencies are local offices which are intended to be staffed by one's trusted peers and neighbors from among the local community. If one does not know one's respective federal agent or officer, the situation is predominately a problem of local government.

A federal income tax essentially places artisans and laborers into real bondage, either by the recursive force of their own disposition as underwriters in good faith of the currency, or by their roles as guarantors of the dollar by right of their election to use it. Ironically, such an arbitrary taxation policy encumbers the workforce with the very tool which is intended to advocate the vested citizenry's immanence of at-large civil agency (or liberty) at the individual level. The practice results in a currency tool which is less effective if not wholly ineffective in its intended use. It also removes from the workforce its constitutionally affirmed and protected natural right not to be robbed or otherwise bonded without due cause.

Taxation without representation engenders a non-egalitarian class dynamic in a marketplace, and it brings about a de facto disposition of adversity among otherwise peer entities. Operators are forced to arrange themselves about a forensic bright line that correlates to derelict accounting practices. Gray-area operator behaviors and self-serving bureaucratic cottage industries flourish.

Because certain discrepancies may be said to have been sustained for long years does not necessarily represent cause for continuance. There are entities inclined to take advantage of the economic dynamics that manifest as a result of such policy. Such cottage industries debauch the currency, cripple the economy, and disenfranchise from its efficacy all who are vested in the American dollar.

With that, the dollar gets hijacked and very easily a local or regional economy can be unseated along with it. From a perspective of any working criminal organization, it really is that simple.

To wit, 1) establish or enjoin derelict or cottage industry operations, 2) locate or create a victim demographic which is unaware of its rights and protections, and 3) misappropriate the currency as a mode of business, e.g., profiteering/racketeering. Such in-bad-faith (or snowblind) operations may seek out a community where there preexists full sunlight among the marketplace right-of-way, and well-established protocols and local precedent for successful relief against such bad operators, simply to avail themselves of the good faith presumptions associated with the local marketplace standard.

Moreover, when there is arbitrary taxation the logistics and leylines of tax assessment, payment, and related market policies get hyper-politicized. There emerges a situation wherein people determine to cope with the situation by implementing and navigating unwritten jungle-rules protocols that necessitate the use of blind alleys and derelict marketplace agents for their operational coverage and oversight. However, it is critical that such bureaucratic cottage industries, because of their implied status of being sanctioned by the governing standard of economic policy under the official rule of law (the presumption of which exposes the public to liability for any vested operator's efforts in bad faith), be brought into conformance with the national standard that is the law of the land. If such operators cannot be corrected then they must be eliminated.

Arbitrary taxation increases scarcity and disparity in the distribution of wealth, which in turn contribute to the domestic and foreign commodification of the dollar wherein it comes into use predominately as an object of wealth or vanity rather than a shared tool among members of a given community or federal jurisdiction. That is, it contributes to profiteering, which is a kind of racketeering, which is a crime.

I am a college-educated journalist, writer, author, media and communications professional, reporter, and investigator who has spent his entire professional career working at publishing operations of some form or another. Venues include newspaper, magazine, digital content, audio, and book production; as well as working in corporate, public, institutional, and faith-based communications roles. I have been a content creator and content carrier in some capacity or another for some fifteen years, during which time I also have cohabitated professionally with the sister arts of publishing that are marketing, advertising, public relations, and circulation. Thereby, I witness the following: in any marketplace, regardless of whether the content is editorial or advertisement, or any other flavor of various marketing distribution or information campaigns; that while the content may be contrived to appear random or incidental, it never is. The black market is no exception. Any such solicitation, if it is reaching any person, is occurring because he or she has been targeted either as a class or as an individual mark, or both. No solicitation is accidental, or even incidental. Information is power, and the media, in these modern times, can have the same access to the technological, intellectual, and economic tools of hegemony as do institutions for applied research, science, engineering, and technology. Such a lucrative landscape presents tempting opportunities in the marketplace, which unfortunately, are taken advantage of in due course of human nature.

For example, when in the past I have investigated dubious organized fraud by mail, the approach has more or less been the same as occurred in the series of events noted in this civil complaint. The scam typically involves a notification from some initiating party and citing a statute, but with a lack of due civil process in sunlight. This is followed by a third-party financial collection letter from a different geographical jurisdiction, and all of these contacts come from forensically clouded origins and by impersonal way of postal mail. They all bear some known corporate or institutional standard with an affectation of "business as usual," and contain a slightly adversarial if not implicitly threatening tone. I have never received a suspicious solicitation which said "road agent" or "crime syndicate" or "identity thief" or "stalker" or "fishing expedition" in its letterhead.

Specifically regarding the federal income tax, all dialog regarding the subject seems to be at least partially hearsay, and all studies and references tend to be self referential if not self serving. One silver lining, perhaps, to this apparently highly variable disposition regarding the matter, could be that it is a reflection of a diverse variety of implementations of local democratic rule of law among the great multiplicity of American jurisdictions. However, one downside to the lack of consensus is that most parties involved in historical litigation on the matter have potentially been agents of a cottage industry, such as, arguably, the Sixty-First Congress which authored and adopted the Sixteenth Amendment to the United States Constitution.

Because I happen to incidentally observe H&R Block store-front locations occupying every neighborhood where I have resided since I first used their tax service some ten years ago does not mean that the corporation is unaware that I reside in various of their local spheres of operation. And because National Public Radio broadcasts a cute news feature each year in April about the federal income tax deadline, does not mean that the program occurs without the organization's principle knowledge that it is serving its listeners with what are generally received to be reminders of time-sensitive ultimatums. It creates a sensation of being hunted by a non-governmental organization in one's own home and community.

Because the Respondent had access to, and evidently used, specific information about my personal and business operations, e.g., calendar, address, individually identifying government data, and financial information, does not necessarily mean that the Respondent, even if acting alone or on deep background, has any right to possess or to act upon any combination of the information. Additionally, the situation is arguably a violation of my various rights to privacy.

Although counsel for the Respondent may argue that the Respondent is operating peaceably as a government bureaucrat, it nevertheless does not entitle the Respondent to any moral or ethical high ground. The Respondent is furthering the interests of such aforementioned cottage industries and market practices, which are out of step with the law's ethics, prevailing logic, and constitutional protections. Such actions are to the direct detriment of American capitalism, and the nation's free markets, and the common wealth of the citizenry.

Often, an agent is unaware of his or her role as the lynch pin of such an operation. This reflects a well-known and frequently abused aspect of bureaucratic compartmentalization of power that can be manipulated to systemically hold harmless or give operational or political quarter to the offending organization, while the actual civil transgression or unconstitutional egress is executed. The problem here is that such agency is not intended to be cognitively separate from the role and duties of any individual citizen. However, for such an end-run scheme to occur, the "official capacity" must trump or be separated from that of the individual's civil agency. Such division violates the spirit of republican self government in the United States wherein the public agency naturally enjoins that of the official. Ironically, such individual civil agency is the actual sole source of official authority under the law.

Such an operational scheme further illumines an aspect of a self-serving cottage industry whose presence is also a key reason why this complaint is filed not against the "national agency" as an organization, but names the individual agent.

To wit, 1) the agent is the agency, in essence and in fact, by all philosophical definitions, to include constitutional context and therefore, in application of the law. As an individual the agent bears both the federal standard as well as the risk and consequences of exposure to civil liability, such as potential vacation of executive incorporation or removal of other incumbency to vested authority, that would normally be brought to bear in response to any violation of rights or liberties occurring through or by the individual's capacity as a human agent, regardless of whether the act is public or private. Also, as these observations illumine a cottage industry which arguably relies on a misunderstanding of the vested powers, or the misapplication of policy if not criminal methods, this complaint names the individual and not the organization, because

2) the Petitioner has no reasonable expectation that the national agency, due to its purported operational disposition, has any inclination or ability to meet the Petitioner's and / or the government's expectations to achieve due process in this matter.

Verily,
C.G. Braswell

RICO, FCA, and Title 42

January 5, 2015

IN THE UNITED STATES DISTRICT COURT
FOR THE DISTRICT OF ARIZONA

(Case Number 4:14-CV-02574-TUC-JAS)

I. Individual Civil Agency; Defrauding the Government

The vesting clauses (*Article I, Section 1, Clause 1; Article II, Section 1, Clause 1; Article III Section 1*) are instructive with respect to the civil faculty of an incorporated citizen. The language is straightforward that the lawmaking powers of the people are vested in the Legislative Branch, and the official powers of the people are vested in the Executive Branch, and the legalistic powers of the people are vested in the Judicial Branch. There is no legitimate means by which a United States government official would arbitrarily contact a law-abiding, peaceable citizen in good standing, to say in essence "you will do this with your property or your wealth, or else you will suffer the government-imposed punishment." Any person who does such a thing is out of order, regardless of whether or not they understand why, and, regardless of any of their affiliations or associations.

The powers vested in the three branches of the Federal Government are an extension of the cognitive faculty which is to be preeminent of course, in the function of any individual who is performing an official U.S. government duty of any sort. An individual who faces an ethical challenge such as was evidently faced by the Respondent [redacted], regardless of whether the human agent is functioning in an official capacity or not, has nevertheless an official duty and a civil obligation to preempt such a violation of the vested citizenry. This would be a localized example of an executive check, which all citizens in good standing have an obligation and responsibility to execute in such a circumstance. The federal executive *agency* is incumbent in such situations, and the role of the chief executive office is an intellectual tool which serves to advocate on behalf of the citizenry in all such instances.

The Supreme Court's considerations in ***Allison Engine v. United States, 553 U.S 07-214 (2008)*** provide a logical analog of the nuances of vested civil capacity or agency in an individual human agent, in juxtaposition with the statutory notion of a U.S. official; Furthermore *Allison* does so among a convenient context of bright-line questions about government fraud. In *Allison*, former subcontractor employees sought relief under provisions of the False Claims Act (***U.S. Code › Title 31 › Subtitle 37 › Subchapter III › § 3729***), citing misrepresentation by one of the litigants, to the United States Navy regarding, fulfillment of contracts financed and compensated by the Treasury. The *Allison* opinion reiterates that:

"The False Claims Act imposes civil liability on any person who knowingly uses a 'false record or statement to get a false or fraudulent claim paid or approved by the government' *[§ 3729 (a)(2)]*, and any person who 'conspires to defraud the Government by getting a false or fraudulent claim allowed or paid'," *§ 3729 (2)(3)*.

"We hold that it is insufficient for a plaintiff asserting a *§ 3729(a)(2)* claim to show merely that 'the false statement's use … resulted in obtaining or getting payment or approval of the claim,' or that 'government money was used to pay the false or fraudulent claim.' Instead, a plaintiff asserting a *3729(a)(2)* claim must prove that the defendant intended that the false record or statement be material to the Government's decision to pay or approve the false claim."

Consider the explication, of these sentences from the *Allison* opinion, from a vantage whereby the government is understood as a protocol of an individual's civil agency as a citizen (a portion of the same which, for example, is vested in the three federal branches); The resulting silhouette is a perfect model of, in its purest form, fraud against the U.S. government; which is the fundamental target of the False Claims Act provisions. It happens that this vantage illumines a scope of relief well beyond that of the civil Racketeer Influenced and Corrupt Organizations Act (RICO) provisions noted in the *Braswell* complaint, in light of the potential breadth of the Respondent's operational mode (*see* **U.S. Code › Title 31 › Subtitle 37 › Subchapter III § 3730** *regarding civil actions for false claims; and, § 3729 regarding false claims and liability (with the provisions* **U.S. Code › Title 18 › Part I › Chapter 96,** *and the* **U.S. Code › Title 42 › Chapter 21 › Subchapter 1** *superseding the provision of § 3729(d)*).)

The Petitioner respectfully puts to the court, pray, that one would be hard pressed to find any American capital liquidity which is not privately guaranteed if not also privately controlled (common wealth notwithstanding); Such a situation, even outside of the arguments about the structure of government with respect to ultimate vested authority, paints such efforts as the Respondent's and her ad hoc associates, in a highly questionable operational role; It captures the Respondent amid some effort of investigation about whether the individuals whom she solicits for collections are politically aware, and, where they are found to be ignorant regarding their liberties, or misinformed due to propaganda in the at-large marketplace of ideas, then the collections effort proceeds, and ultimately a claim gets paid pursuant to some initial statement being made to the targeted individual. As required for FCA complaints as the court held in *Allison*, a dependency upon the initial statement or claim must be established, which is a logical assessment for *Braswell*. Also, the Respondent's mode of operation seems to go further to establish intent to transgress (if not an act of outright mockery of the vested civil status).

II. Ad Hoc Operators and Civil R.I.C.O. Relief

Activities such as fraud and theft are widely and historically known, and there is a wide range of options for relief from their perpetrators, though most of them are exercises in criminal procedure; However this complaint is brought to bear in this court because the perceived problems are, at least in part, resulting from difficulties at the federal policy-making level related to local enforcement (***Guarantee Clause***, ***Article IV Section 4)***. Excepting any voluntary basis, for anyone or any organization to appropriate some arbitrary portion of wealth or property from any other person or any group, without due process (***Fifth Amendment***), is against the law. The Respondent evidently had access to, and used, specific information about the Petitioner's personal and business operations, such as his day calendar, residential address, individually identifying government and personal data, and financial information; However that does not mean that the Respondent, even if acting alone or on deep investigative background, has any right to act upon or even possess any combination of the information *(per Fourth Amendment privacy protections and unenumerated Ninth Amendment protections; with supporting statutory relief via U.S. Code › Title 18 › Part I › Chapter 96 › § 1961 (1)(A) (extortion); (1)(B) (extortionate credit transactions re: penalty rate in letter from Austin); and relating to fraud and related activity in connection with access devices or in connection with identification documents, re: egressing Petitioner's personal information; and mail fraud; and financial institution fraud re: penalty interest rate noted in collections letter from Austin; and relating even to peonage re: ostensible recurring identity theft and contributing to ongoing, years-long systemic violations of the same type against Petitioner).*

Examples of fraud by way of the mail, or fraud by misapplication of a standard-bearing entity, or through fraudulent financial claims all share a common aspect; That is the use of paper tools; or as the common law has it, by some writ of authority. Any such illegitimate writs are naturally constructed to be viewed as purporting actual authority *bona fide.* (**Writs of Attainder** do not explicitly notify the recipient or the affected parties by way of declaring "this is an outright Bill of Goods.")

The Petitioner is cautious about invoking any misunderstandings by the court, that his complaint targets anyone except the Respondent in the Respondent's personal, intellectual, cognitive, and legalistic capacity as an individual human agent and U.S. citizen, for failure to fulfill her vested obligations thereof. Challenges of Bills of Attainder (*Article I, Section 9, Clause Three*), while they are excellent fundamental models for illustrating fraudulent institutional mechanisms, nevertheless most often reach the federal courts consequent to some legislated rule, so application of the law thereby frequently occurs at an organizational level; (The same imminent point can be easily made regarding, the ***Thirteenth Amendment***'s abolition of slavery and involuntary servitude and the ***Fourteenth Amendment*** exception for state actor/state action with respect to the **Abolition** (ensuing **Black Codes** notwithstanding the exception). To wit, by the Federal rule of law, regarding violations of civil liberties, actual civil and criminal transgressions both, are said to occur at the hand of the actor in fact *(see **U.S. Code** › **Title 42** › **Chapter 21** › **Subchapter 1 § 1985(3) § 1986**, regarding action for neglect to prevent violations of civil rights).*

Therefore, the Respondent should not be allowed to succeed in invoking any "official capacity" defense to seek political quarter for the Respondent's actions; as *Braswell* herein establishes that the Respondent's duties and operations are unconstitutional and in violation of the Petitioner's due process and privacy protections affirmed in the ***Fourth Amendment*** and ***Fifth Amendment*** as well as various unenumerated provisions of the ***Ninth Amendment;*** as well as ***Tenth Amendment*** reaffirmations such as with respect to the civil power vested in the Petitioner to bring this action, as well as the Respondent's vested civil capacity, which capitally obligates her to intercede such a transgression(s) that she instead put upon the Petitioner explicitly *(see **U.S. Code** › **Title 42** › **Chapter 21** › **Subchapter 1 § 1983** regarding provisions for civil action for deprivation of civil rights).*

So, keeping in mind the aforementioned caveats regarding responsibilities for individual cognitive agency, as it relates to bright-line transgression of civil liberties, that may occur through the wielding of a seemingly authoritative writ; the disposition of the United States Court of Appeals for the Second Circuit in ***Acorn v. United States**, **09-5172-cv and 10-0992-cv (2010)**,* reiterates the identification of the three elements that amount to a Bill of Attainder, to wit:

(1) "specification of the affected persons," (2) "punishment" and (3) "lack of judicial trial."

Braswell v. [redacted] argues that 1) the Petitioner is specifically affected in his liberties by the Defendant's fraudulent collection efforts, in a 2) punitive sense as it disenfranchises the Petitioner from his individual civil sovereignty in good standing and even as a taxpayer, inasmuch as it disrupts his free application or disposal of his real or intellectual property in the due course of his role as a head of household, a business owner, and an American citizen, and thereby, Petitioner suffers the consequences of a non-egalitarian 3) de facto class action adjudication, by writ *(see text **Sixteenth Amendment**)* implemented by the, erstwhile with all due respect, Sixty-First Congress of the United States *(again, **U.S. Code › Title 42 › Chapter 21 › Subchapter 1 § 1988 (a)**, regarding applicability of statutory or common law for proceedings in vindication of civil rights).*

The Respondent, failing the foremost obligation of the Respondent's purported capacity as a vested government official, to put into check such an unconstitutional operation, therefore is liable by right of the Respondent's natural agency as an individual *(see **U.S. Code › Title 42 › Chapter 21 › Subchapter 1 § 1983** regarding provisions for civil action for deprivation of civil rights).*

Anza v. Ideal Steel, 547 U.S. 04-433 (2006) provides a vantage from the Supreme Court regarding application of the Racketeer Influenced and Corrupt Organizations Act, wherein the Supreme Court has been inclined towards establishing proximate cause rather than "but-for" causality, as defendants in the case argued:

"that RICO's private right of action must be interpreted in light of common-law principals, and that at common law a fraud action requires the plaintiff to prove reliance. Because Ideal has not satisfied the proximate-cause requirement articulated in *Holmes,* we have no occasion to address the substantial question whether a showing of reliance is required."

Braswell argues reliance in addition to proximate cause. Without the letter from the Respondent, the Petitioner would have had no natural compulsion to tender payment, therefore, the ensuing sequence of events occurred as a direct result of the Respondent's solicitation. And the Petitioner relied upon the information to the extent that he paid the amount that was solicited by the Respondent, after the sum was communicated to the Petitioner along with a letter denying his "application for extension of time for payment of tax due to undue hardship." The Respondent's letter sought the same amount as was sought by the financial collections document mailed to the Petitioner from Austin, Texas, that additionally assessed a 0.5% penalty rate to the outstanding amount. Braswell payed the amount demanded, in person at a physical location, where he went through an electronically-invasive security checkpoint staffed by *lethally-armed guards*, where he (and his eight-year-old son) were also *ordered to remove their shoes and belt and empty the contents of their pockets*. Such historically clamorous displays of institutionalized "public" force among the cottage industry which surrounds federal income tax collection, reinforces the

Petitioner's inclination to rely on the tax collector's willingness and ability to command collection.

One of the reasons Petitioner Braswell is in pro se is, because during two separate consultations with Phoenix-area attorneys, both lawyers characterized such a case as *Braswell v.* [redacted] to be legalistically futile, and both of them indicated that such an action would be viewed in a negative light by those among their respective bar associations, and, both stated that such an effort on the Petitioner's part would result in a real threat to the complainant's person, family, and liberty. With that, such an ad hoc political display of private complicity with the cottage industry that surrounds so-called federal income tax collection, also reinforces the Petitioner's estimation regarding the political willingness and boots-on-the-ground ability of the tax collector and her ad hoc organization to collect on the amount solicited.

Anza also addresses certain nuances with respect to the willingness, complicity, awareness, and intent of the business-end agent of an alleged racketeering operation or other criminal syndicate (such as would conceivably include the degree to which "private investigations" were applied by the Respondent's operation), in the light of the original intent of the RICO provisions (***U.S. Code › Title 18 › Part I › Chapter 96 › § 1962(a)(b)(c)*** *regarding prohibited activities enforceable under the Racketeer Influenced and Corrupt Organizations Act*) to eliminate the infiltration of organized crime and racketeering into legitimate organizations operating in interstate commerce.

Regarding investigations, privacy, and a reasonable expectation for freedom to implement one's day-to-day means, it is worth noting that since 2002, the Petitioner in *Braswell v.* [redacted] has been a working journalist, in the due course of which he regularly provides reportage and collaborates with local government, federal officials, and law enforcement agencies in multiple states (most frequently pro bono) and conducts civil and other legalistic discovery to include credentialed public and private investigations. At this point in his career, the Petitioner realizes that certain means by which certain governmental and non-governmental organizations, and privately held corporations, and otherwise operators of a particular class or disposition, use questionable means, which regularly transgress American civil liberties; and, which impede the Petitioner's ability to negotiate sensitive sources, to guarantee confidentiality, and to sufficiently implement his own effective forensic protocols, et cetera, while at the same time attending to the ongoing safety of himself and his family, as well as contributing to that of the ambient community at large. As noted editorially in the *Petitioner's Brief No. 1*, the protocol implemented by the Respondent and the Respondent's interstate associates is indistinguishable from some of the more flagrant in-bad-faith market operators such as those who repeatedly hound victims for mail-based collections. Also, after fifteen years in his current vocational mode, it becomes increasingly clear to the Petitioner that such operators are out of order, regardless of their umbrella affiliation or logo, and that they do indeed continue to victimize people wherever they are not formally and firmly interdicted.

Anza weighs consideration regarding a syndicate's "use and investment of racketeering proceeds, 'as distinct from injury traceable simply to the predicate acts of racketeering alone or to the conduct of the business of the enterprise'." While it is not clear how Petitioner Braswell's individual "tax dollars" were or are to be appropriated, locally or otherwise (although there are some somewhat speculative nationwide percentages published by the Office of the President of the United

States), the amount paid by the Petitioner in 2014 (and all previous years) is a known quantity. *Anza* also makes an affirmation about compensable injury *(see **U.S. Code › Title 18 › Part I › Chapter 96 › § 1964c** regarding provisions for civil remedies)*, that correlates civil liability with the footprint of a pattern:

"(citing *Sedima*) necessarily is the harm caused by predicate acts sufficiently related to constitute a pattern, for the essence of the violation is the commission of those acts in connection with the conduct of an enterprise."

These items have implications regarding the ambient scope of the Respondent's operation and therefore implications regarding the path ahead for discovery in *Braswell (please reference government investigative protocols stipulated in the following rules: **U.S. Code › Title 18 › Part I › Chapter 96 › § 1968 (a)(f1)(f3)(f4)(f5) (f6)(g)(i)(j)** regarding civil investigative demand; also **U.S. Code › Title 18 › Part I › Chapter 96 › § 1967** regarding evidence presented in court)*. *Anza* also notes the subject of indictable mail fraud *(see **18 U.S. Code › Title 18 Part I › Chapter 63 ›§ 1341** provisions defining frauds and swindles)* as a RICO investigation qualifier.

Copies of the complaint in the *Braswell* qui tam action were provided to the United States Attorney General in The District of Columbia *(see **U.S. Code › Title 18 › Part I › Chapter 96 › § 1965** regarding venue and process; and **U.S. Code › Title 18 › Part I › Chapter 96 › § 1964(a)** regarding civil remedies)*, as well as to the United States Attorney General for the District of Arizona, in Tucson *(see **U.S. Code › Title 18 › Part I › Chapter 96 › § 1964(b)(d)** regarding civil remedies; and **U.S. Code ›***

*Title 18 › Part I › Chapter 96 › § 1968 (a)(c)(f)(g)(h)
regarding civil investigative demand, and **U.S. Code ›
Title 18 › Part I › Chapter 96 › § 1966** regarding
expedition of actions; and **U.S. Code › Title 42 › Chapter
21 › Subchapter 1 § 1988(a)(b)(c)** regarding proceedings
in vindication of civil rights.)*

*(Also regarding procedure for potential consideration of
relief under provisions of the False Claims Act, see **U.S.
Code › Title 31 › Subtitle 37 › Subchapter III › § 3731**
regarding false claims procedure; **§ 3732** regarding false
claims jurisdiction; and **§ 3733** regarding civil
investigative demands for false claims. (In **§ 3729**,
regarding false claims and liability, the provisions of **U.S.
Code › Title 18 › Part I › Chapter 96,** and the **U.S. Code ›
Title 42 › Chapter 21 › Subchapter 1** supersede that of §
3729(d).)*

III. Economic Landscape and Marketplace Opportunity

Activities such as those with which the Respondent is
involved are more widely effective and successful in
marketplace environments where the rights and liberties of
the community members are not clearly trumpeted. The
Respondent is named as an individual, and not in the
Respondent's official capacity, as discussed above;
However, the following economic situations noted below
(in addition to the situations conducive to cottage
industries as summarized in *Petitioner's Brief No. 1,*
contribute to the ambient clamor and general lack of
clarity that enable such in-bad-faith schemes as
illegitimate tax collection operations which operate under
an Executive seal, to take hold and thrive in a given
community, apparently repeatedly victimizing various
groups and individuals (illustrating another ethical

compulsion for Braswell's complaint; that is, as an action brought due to a civil obligation to "stop and render aid," as it were).

There remains optimistic expectations that the Congress understands its power of the purse in the context of the United States' economy in the twenty-first century, however, regional "financial institutions" are also key contributors to manifestations of off-the-mark de facto policy, and to the emergence of parasitic financial cottage industries by which all in-good-faith marketplace operators are negatively impacted.

A representative array of such regional operators who over-hedge on the dollar, as a sort of vanity or as a commodity and status symbol of wealth, rather than focusing their applications of, and their marketplace interactions with the dollar as a tool, capitally, have recently found their constitutional separation-of-powers and due process arguments against progressive policy such as the Federal Reserve System, to have been dispatched in the U.S. District Court for the District of Columbia in ***State National Bank of Big Spring v. Jacob J. Lew 1:12-cv-01032-ESH (2013)***. Therein, the court, in essence, upheld an interpretation that Federal Reserve Notes are a tool, not a vanity or status symbol, therefore even states cannot have a real "property right" to any such manifestation on paper of such a policy or statute:

"However, the Court is unconvinced that the States have a present injury because the States' underlying premise that they have a "property right" in the configuration of the Bankruptcy Code is flawed. Simply put, the States' holding of certain statutory rights does not amount to an inalienable property right under the Bankruptcy Code."

That is, one cannot cash a bill, and one cannot use money as food, and a state must view the federal currency as statute not property. Furthermore, the court essentially put forth, that from a national perspective (that is, the general federal administrative realm which includes the U.S. Treasury and the Federal Reserve System), the administration of the dollar is one that must be as quick and essential for use in liquidating assets as it can be for underwriting them, and with such decisions wholly governed by the greater best interest of the vested citizenry rather than being influenced by any accumulated quantity of cash value or individual or regional status of privilege or wealth in dollars:

"...orderly liquidation authority could be used if and only if the failure of the financial company would threaten U.S. financial stability."

Optimism about the Legislature notwithstanding, disorientation regarding federal fiscal policy as applied in local jurisdictions is evident, presumably due to a lack of cohesion at the institutional level for the administration of various funding mechanisms which are available to all three branches of the federal government, and resulting in myriad economic consequences (*for example, see **General Order 13-21 for the United States District Court for the District of Arizona,** filed October 9, 2013, regarding the impasse between the Legislative Branch and the Executive Branch of the United States, with respect to funding for its Judicial Branch*).

About one hundred and two years ago, and some ten months after the adoption of the Sixteenth Amendment in the year 1913, when the **Federal Reserve Act** was signed into law (***U.S. Code › Title 12 › Chapter 3 › Subchapter IX › § 341,*** *general enumeration of powers for the Federal Reserve System*), the would-be official status of the Respondent was formally mooted, barring the Respondent's democratic election as a federal income tax collector in the local jurisdiction. As was necessary, such behavior as the Respondent's, as a class, was again restrained with the formal abolition of peonage in 1957 (***U.S. Code › Title 42 › Chapter 21 › Subchapter 1 § 1994***).